SMITHSONIAN INSTITUTION
WAR BACKGROUND STUDIES
NUMBER FOUR

PEOPLES *of the* PHILIPPINES

By

HERBERT W. KRIEGER

(PUBLICATION 3694)

CITY OF WASHINGTON
PUBLISHED BY THE SMITHSONIAN INSTITUTION
NOVEMBER 13, 1942

The Lord Baltimore Press
BALTIMORE, MD., U. S. A.

CONTENTS

ILLUSTRATIONS

PLATES

TEXT FIGURES

PEOPLES OF THE PHILIPPINES

By HERBERT W. KRIEGER

Curator of Ethnology, U. S. National Museum

(WITH 24 PLATES)

THE LAND AND ITS PEOPLE

Most Americans have observed individual Filipinos going about their business, as student, taxi driver, domestic servant, gardener, politician, or journalist—90,000 aliens in an alien land. Many of us have learned to distinguish the general appearance of the Filipino from other Orientals—the Japanese, the Korean, and the Chinese. As a people we have come to recognize with emotion the classic features of the President of the Commonwealth of the Philippines, Manuel L. Quezon, whose ancestry is half Spanish, and of the Commonwealth's Vice President, Sergio Osmeña, whose ancestry is in part Chinese. They typify to us the traditional leadership of those of mixed blood, either Spanish or Chinese, the so-called mestizo classes, who enjoyed the advantages of rearing in families whose economic conditions were far above mere subsistence levels. Less well known to the American public is the short-statured, suave, good-natured, English-speaking, pure-blood Filipino typified by such men as Col. Carlos P. Romulo, who, before the irruption of the Japanese, published the leading English daily newspaper in Manila, won a Pulitzer prize in journalism, and in the defense of his country revealed great heroism in Bataan. Although the Filipino is for the most part nominally Catholic in his religious beliefs, we know him best as a political protestant—protesting his desire for immediate and complete national independence. His acculturation to the principles and surface manifestations of modern western civilization is increasingly apparent, despite three centuries of indoctrination in Spanish customs and traditions and many centuries more of Arabic and Hindu influences. Indonesian culture survivals are, however, everywhere manifest in his daily life, beliefs, thoughts, and actions.

Only slight differences in physical appearance and structure are observable between the southern Chinese, the Perak Malay, and the Filipino peoples taken as a unit. With the exception of the Philippine pygmy Negrito, the Filipino has typical Mongoloid characteristics such as straight, coarse, black hair, smooth skin, slight hirsute development and practically no beard. His delicate bone structure, short stature, graceful body, brown

1

skin and other minor physical criteria establish the Filipino as a member of the same widespread east Asiatic race that is widely disseminated throughout southern China, the Malay Peninsula, Sumatra, Java, Borneo, and the entire island world encompassing the southeastern Asiatic coast, geographically designated Indonesia.

A useful classification of the native population of the Philippine Islands introduced by the Spanish shortly after the conquest included three main elements: negrillos, indios, and moros. The negrillos, or small black people, whose average stature is less than 5 feet, are now known to us as Negritos. The indios (Indians) and moros (Moors) embraced the majority, since the number of Negritos was small even in 1565. The distinction existing between indios and moros as understood by the Spanish invader was purely cultural. The peaceful, agricultural, pagan peoples occupying the coastal plains and the valleys of Luzon and the Visayas were indios; the aggressive, pirating, slave-hunting, marauding proselytes of Islam, established in Jolo, Mindanao, and minor coastal settlements on Mindoro, Lubang, and even on the shores of Manila Bay at the mouth of the Pasig River, were soon known to the Spanish as "moros" in remembrance of their ancient Arabic Mohammedan antagonists in Spain and in North Africa, the Moors.

The coastal and valley pagan Filipino peoples were soon converted to Christianity. As the Spaniards extended their knowledge of the Islands' peoples to the wild tribes of the upland interior, they encountered a fourth ethnic element that resisted conversion and remained conservatively pagan. These peoples were named "infieles" (unbelievers or heathens). They remain essentially pagan peoples, "wild tribes," to the present day.

This classification of the peoples of the Philippines was reached through common observation of prevailing differences in native cultures and adaptability to Spanish civilization and Christianity. It remains the popularly accepted classification of native ethnic groups and has also been taken over by those physical anthropologists who believe they have observed an underlying subracial difference supposedly existing between the lowland agricultural peoples and the wild mountain tribes, the unbelievers, "infieles" of the Spanish. In so doing the terms "Malay" and "Indonesian" have been bandied about.

The "Malay," a distinct people, originally living in north Sumatra, and numbering actually only a small fraction of the total population of Indonesia, is represented in the Philippines only through small accretions and minor immigrant groups. The Moro is a Malayan primarily through having adopted the Malay's way of living, his Mohammedan religion, and

FIG. 1.—Peoples of the Philippines.

his Arabic alphabet. The Moro people has grown in numbers primarily through slave-taking expeditions in the several Philippine Islands, from Mindanao north to Luzon. The Moro population is therefore ethnically quite mixed, essentially Filipino and not at all Malayan. Much less are the sedentary, agricultural Filipino peoples Malays, since they have not adopted Malay culture and have received few Malay immigrants. The prestige of the Malay has been such as to induce anthropologists to designate the Christian Filipino "Malay." The pagan Filipino peoples have been arbitrarily designated "Indonesians," borrowing a geographical term, although the physical specifications of this so-called subrace vary according to the author cited.

Those Indonesian islands which the Spanish in 1565 named "the Philippines," in honor of their King Philip II, lie off the coast of southeastern Asia directly across the China Sea, 500 miles east of Hong Kong and the Chinese province of Kuan-Tung, and 600 miles east of Saigon, the seaport of French Indo-China.

The Islands are situated between 21°10' and 4°40' north latitude and between 116°40' and 126°34' east longitude. There are altogether 7,083 islands in the archipelago, which extends 1,150 statute miles from north to south and 682 miles from east to west. Only 462 islands have an area of 1 square mile or over. The area of the entire archipelago is approximately 115,600 square miles, or slightly less than the combined land areas of Pennsylvania, Maryland, Virginia, and West Virginia. However, less than 15 percent of its surface is under cultivation. Although the population of the Philippines is primarily agricultural, it is very unevenly distributed. In the densely populated river valleys of central Luzon and in the centrally located Visayan Islands, the average size of a Filipino farm is only 3 acres, while the upland plains country in the vicinity of Lake Lanao in northern Mindanao is but sparsely occupied.

The largest islands are Luzon, in the north, which covers a land area of 40,814 square miles, and Mindanao, in the south, with an area of 36,906 square miles. The so-called Visayan or Bisayan islands occupying a central position between these two great islands are much smaller in area but are nevertheless important. Five of them, namely, Samar, with an area of 5,124 square miles, Negros, with 4,904, Panay, with 4,445, Palawan, with 4,500, and Mindoro, with 3,794 square miles, each have a greater land area than Puerto Rico, while the smaller Visayan islands of Cebu, Bohol, and Masbate each are approximately one-half its size.

The great island mass southwest of Asia, which we know as Indonesia, includes, from north to south, Formosa; the Philippines; the Greater

1. SANTA MESA ROAD

A countryside in the vicinity of Manila. Characteristic features are the papaya tree (right), the banana, and the tall bamboo (center), the thatched roofs of the houses, the open walls with sliding shutters, the small translucent shell panes, the rutted, unsurfaced road, and the fence of bamboo pickets.

2. A FLOODED STREET IN MANILA

During the summer rainy season, winds of hurricane force pile up the waters of Manila Bay onto its low flat shore lands. Filipinos go about their business as usual knowing from experience that the waters will soon subside.

1. THE BRIDGE OF SPAIN—PUENTA ESPAÑOL, 1896

This ancient Spanish masterpiece of flat arch construction in stone spanned the Pasig River at Manila and connected the walled city with the business district. Twice damaged by earthquakes it has been replaced by a reinforced concrete structure, popularly known as the "Bridge Jones."

2. PUERTA DE ISABEL II

One of the gates in the massive walls of the Intramuros, or walled city of Manila, rebuilt by Spain for the third time in 1863. The walls and gates remain for the most part intact although heavily bombed by the Japanese.

1. Casco, or Freight Barge, Landing at Corregidor Island

Freight traffic on the Pasig River and Manila Bay is still moved by stout barges of this character. The large flexible basketry deck covers, the cumbersome rudder, also the magic eye painted on its sides are characteristic.

2. A Double Outrigger Coasting Banca at Anchor

This seaworthy, round-bottom type of sailing boat carries a square-rigged sail and is the traditional means of interisland travel.

1. THREE CARABAO CARTS

The carabao or water buffalo remains the common carrier and beast of burden throughout the archipelago. Automotive trucks are too expensive for general use, and the native horse is unreliable and too small for use as a draft animal.

2. CARCAR-BARILI ROAD, CEBU ISLAND

Cebu is the most densely inhabited island in the Philippines. Here the cultivation of rice has been superseded by that of maize. Former cropping in the hilly uplands has resulted in erosion of the soil leaving bare hills. Note the cornfield in the foreground.

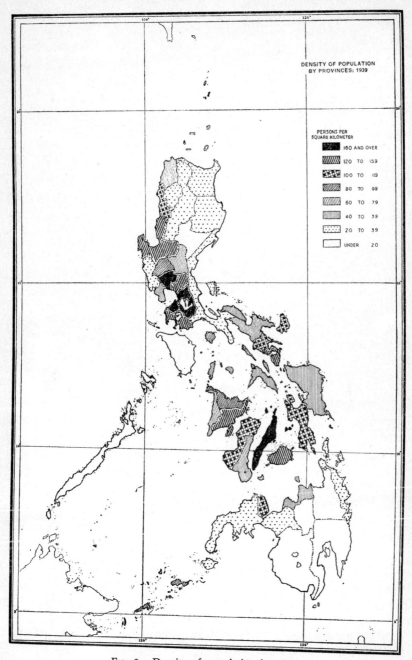

DENSITY OF POPULATION
BY PROVINCES: 1939

PERSONS PER
SQUARE KILOMETER

160 AND OVER
120 TO 159
100 TO 119
80 TO 99
60 TO 79
40 TO 59
20 TO 39
UNDER 20

FIG. 2.—Density of population in 1939.

Sunda islands of Sumatra, Java, Borneo, and Celebes; the Lesser Sunda islands east of Java from Bali to Timor; the small islands between this chain and New Guinea, known as the Southeastern and Southwestern Islands; and the Moluccas, a vast number of islands, large and small, in the Banda and Moluccas Seas between Celebes and New Guinea.

The population of the Dutch East Indies, which includes most of these islands except the Philippines, together with British Borneo and Portuguese Timor, is 58,000,000. The population of the Philippines, according to the census of 1940, is 16,350,000. Java alone has a population of about 40,000,000, with a density of 800 per square mile. But Sumatra, a much larger island, has a population density of only 42 per square mile, while Borneo has 9, Celebes 59, the Lesser Sundas 100, and the Moluccas 12. The Philippine archipelago, with its 16,350,000 people and a land area of 115,600 square miles, has a density of 143 per square mile, which, as indicated, is very unevenly distributed.

The Philippine archipelago is roughly wedge-shaped with its apex pointing to the north and extending at its base on the south in submerged mountain ranges which reappear in the islands of Borneo, Celebes, and Gilolo or Halmahera. The northern apex extends northward beyond the great island of Luzon in a chain of small islands, the Babuyanes and Batanes. Geographically, the large island of Formosa, which lies northward of these small island chains and which is visible from the Batanes, should, properly speaking, be included with the Philippine archipelago since the same axial mountain range, the Sierra Madre, that extends from one end of the archipelago to the other, from southern Mindanao along the east coast of Luzon, also forms the eastern elevated portion of Formosa, although that island has been separated from the Philippines since the early Tertiary, in geologic times. At this northern apex the waters separating it from the mainland of China narrow to a deep channel. The submerged mountain range here veers to the northeast in the direction of the Liukiu Islands, south of Japan.

The axial mountain system traversing the entire Philippine archipelago along its eastern extremity is continued on the south along the base of the ocean floor in a southeasterly direction reappearing again to form the little-known island of Halmahera, which is traversed by the Equator, and several other smaller islands. The southwestern peninsula of Mindanao projects southward as a second subterranean mountain range, extending across the ocean floor in a southwesterly direction, and only its peaks appearing above the water, to form the numerous islands of the Sulu or Jolo archipelago. A still more westerly arm at the base of the wedge-shaped Philippine archipelago is formed by the 250-mile long, and exceedingly narrow island of Palawan, until 1906 known as Paragua, where this western range again dips below the surface of the water to form the shallow Balabac Strait, and a number of intervening islands which alone separate the Philippines at this point from the large island of Borneo on the south.

AMERICAN CONTACTS

American interest in the Philippine Islands has varied greatly from year to year. During the early period of our nation's existence, the China trade between New England and Canton served to familiarize our sailors and shipping interests with the commercial products of the Islands. After 1814 when general permission had been given by the Philippine colonial government to foreigners to establish trading posts in Manila, the American flag became conspicuous among the vessels anchored in the waters of Manila Bay. Manila hemp (abacá) for rope making became a trade staple in great demand by the New England ropewalks and shipyards. Crude sugar in earthenware jars (*pilones*) was also purchased in part for home consumption and in part for reexport to Great Britain. In 1858 there were three American export and import establishments in Manila. Later, as other Philippine ports, namely, Iloilo on the island of Panay, Zamboango in western Mindanao, and Cebu on the Visayan island of similar name, midway between Luzon and Mindanao, were opened to foreign traders, exports of Philippine products increased. From Iloilo we received leaf tobacco (Manila wrapper), dyewood (sapan), rope fiber (Manila hemp), obtained from the stem of the abacá plant (*Musa textilis*), which resembles the banana plant, and hides. From Zamboango and the Moro Islands were imported a miscellaneous lot of goods such as tortoise shell, mother-of-pearl (*Haliotis*) or abalone shell, while from Manila came a limited amount of objects reshipped from Chinese, Mexican, and Spanish sources.

American men of science were not far behind our commercial pioneers in developing interests in Philippine research. The United States Exploring Expedition under Lieutenant, later Admiral, Charles Wilkes, received instructions from President Martin Van Buren to explore and survey "the Great Southern Ocean in the important interests of our commerce embarked in the whale fisheries and other adventures in that ocean, as well as to determine the existence of all doubtful islands and shoals, and to discover and accurately fix the position of those which lie in or near the track pursued by our merchant vessels in that quarter." In 1841, after leaving the Hawaiian Islands, two of the Expedition's ships, the

Vincennes and the *Flying Fish,* charted the position of the islands and reefs "laid down as existing on the route towards the East Indies. Only one of them was found to exist, *viz.,* Wakes Island." Guam and the Caroline Islands (Ladrones) were visited, whence the Expedition sailed to the environs of Manila, where waters and coast lines were compared with existing charts.

At Manila, all available charts and sailing information relating to the Sulu Sea were obtained from the Captain of the Port. Commander Wilkes was warned by that official that this information might be erroneous. He was able to correct many inaccuracies in the charts relating to the Straits of Mindoro, a passage 150 miles south of Manila connecting the Sulu and the China Seas.

The vessels of the Exploring Expedition proceeded down the coast of Panay to the Straits of Basilan, thence to the Jolo (Sulu) Archipelago. Here Wilkes received the written promise of the Sultan of Sulu to protect the lives and property of shipwrecked Americans. He also obtained a statement of the terms under which the sultan would receive American ships and permit the handling of their cargoes. Next the Strait of Balabac, between the Philippine island of Palawan and northern Borneo, was charted to facilitate American navigation to China and the Philippines during the "contrary monsoons," that is, the period of southeast prevailing winds in summer and autumn. Wilkes then sailed for Singapore. No ethnological studies of the Philippine people were undertaken, although small ethnographical collections were made in Manila and in Singapore. A very old edition of a Tagalog grammar was obtained, giving details of the use of the native alphabet or syllabary. A collection of plants was made, chiefly in Luzon, which are preserved in various herbaria, notably the United States National Herbarium, Smithsonian Institution. The Exploring Expedition was in Philippine waters from January 13 to February 12, 1842. Available commercial statistics, ethnic and population data were assembled.

During the period extending from 1842 to 1898 routine reports of the American Consul in Manila included important bits of scientific information pertaining to the Filipino people. One of the outstanding reports is that by Consul Alexander R. Webb, issued in 1889, and based apparently entirely on his own observations. Even at that time, in a period long antedating the automobile, American concerns engaged in the export of transportation vehicles. Mr. Webb calls specific attention to the large number of Philadelphia-made carriages and carts to be seen on the streets of Manila.

A group of scientists from the University of Michigan engaged during the seventies and eighties in a biological and botanical exploration of the Islands. One of the expedition's members interested in the collection of botanical and biological specimens was Dean C. Worcester. His intimate knowledge of the people, particularly the non-Christian tribes in northern Luzon, and of the geography of the country gained during this period was later of value to the United States when American civil government was introduced after 1901.

Ethnological studies of the Philippine people appearing in European publications, particularly the conflicting viewpoints of Blumentritt and Hamy, regarding racial classification of the several Filipino peoples were reviewed by American scholars. After 1898 when American interest in the Philippine Islands suddenly became very intense, these monographic studies were briefed or republished in the United States. American scholars now began to publish leaflets and brief summaries regarding the Philippine Islands and its peoples, practically all of which were based on the laborious research of native Filipino, English, German, Spanish, and French scholars. Within a few years, however, there were published in the United States a number of original and scholarly works. The first volumes of a compilation of historical source material edited and annotated by Emma Helen Blair and James Alexander Robinson were published in 1903. The project ultimately included a total of 55 volumes, covering a period of Spanish history extending from the years 1493 to 1803 and gave, in English translation, not only the source material and copies of the original secular and ecclesiastical history of the Philippine Islands during the three centuries following the first visit by Europeans, but also the source documents pertaining to the exploration and colonial administration of the Islands, their geology, biology, and ethnology.

On February 7, 1905, President Theodore Roosevelt, who was always interested in scientific research, addressed the following letter to the Senate and House of Representatives:

Circumstances have placed under the control of this Government the Philippine Archipelago. The islands of that group present as many interesting and novel questions with respect to their ethnology, their fauna and flora, and their geology and mineral resources as any region of the world. At my request the National Academy of Sciences appointed a committee to consider and report upon the desirability of instituting scientific explorations of the Philippine Islands. The report of this committee . . . . accompanies this message.

The scientific surveys which should be undertaken go far beyond any surveys or explorations which the government of the Philippine Islands, however completely self-supporting, could be expected to make. The surveys, while of course beneficial to the people of the Philippine Islands, should be undertaken as a national work for the information not merely of the people of the Philippine Islands, but of the people of this country and of the world. Only preliminary explorations have yet been made in the archipelago, and it should be a matter of pride to the Government of the United States fully to investigate and to describe the entire region. . . . .

This recommendation by the President ultimately resulted in the development of several types of scientific research in the Islands, in part continued by branches of the Federal Government, such as the Coast and Geodetic Survey, and in part entrusted to a newly created Philippine Bureau of Science. The scientific program has many major accomplishments to its credit in ethnology, zoology, forestry, botany, geology, mineral resources, marine hydrography, topography, including a cadastral land survey, and a geodetic and coastal survey.

American scholars and politically-minded people soon reacted from their first naïve acceptance of America as an imperial power and began to write more critically and to be more open-minded regarding the national aspirations of the Philippine people. The thinking public began to appreciate that the United States had inherited a political crisis which had its origin deep in the Spanish colonial policy of the preceding century. The splendid work of our first civil governor, William Howard Taft, did much to remove the agrarian grievances of the Filipino sharecropper. It was later, under President Woodrow Wilson, that the Filipino's second major grievance was removed which, in 1896, 2 years before the coming of the Americans, had led to the Filipino insurrection against Spain. The trained and educated Filipino civil servant was at last given equal opportunity with the American colonial employee. Furthermore, by franchise under a secret ballot, major responsibility in the executive, judicial, and legislative departments of the Philippine insular government became, by law of the American Congress, vested in the Filipino. The American party system with its emphasis on differences, either fancied or real, between the major parties, and the long-drawn-out political discussions in the United States centering on the subject of imperialism, had tended to obscure an important statement of our policy toward the Philippine Islands included in a resolution by the United States Senate February 14, 1899, shortly after the ratification of the peace treaty with Spain which reads as follows:

RESOLVED: That by the ratification of the treaty of peace with Spain it is not intended to incorporate the inhabitants of the Philippine Islands into citizenship of the United States, nor is it intended to permanently annex said Islands as an integral part of the territory of the United States; but it is the intention of the United States to establish on said Islands a government suitable to the wants and conditions of the inhabitants of said Islands, to prepare them for local self-government and in due time to make such disposition of said Islands as will best promote the interests of the citizens of the United States and the inhabitants of said Islands.

Until the close of the insurrection against the American force which lasted for more than 2 years, the government of the Islands was in the control of the United States Army.

In the meantime a Bureau of Insular Affairs in the Department of War was organized in Washington. A commission was appointed by the President to study local conditions in the Philippines and as early as 1901 the Army turned over the government of the Christianized population of the Islands to the first civil governor, William Howard Taft. The then Secretary of War, Elihu Root, was largely responsible for the broad and wise policy of the government established, and from which there has been little departure regardless of the party in power in the United States. This policy won the cooperation of the Filipino. Under President Wilson there was an acceleration in the Filipinization of the insular civil service. This policy, of course, was in line with the major American policy of "The Philippines for the Filipino." Lack of experience and perhaps a certain amount of greed on the part of individual politicians led to inefficiency, particularly in the economic field. To speed up the plan of Filipinization, the United States Congress in 1916 passed the Jones Bill, which placed all legislative powers in the hands of the elected Filipinos and established an elective senate. There had already been established an elective assembly.

The American people, who had at first reacted so enthusiastically to the notion of becoming a power in the Far East, accepted with little show of feeling our retreat from imperialism, the removal of practically all our civil servants from administrative positions in the Islands, and the gradual and finally complete Filipinization of the government of the Islands. America had developed new interests. She could no longer be troubled with problems originating in so apparently remote a place as the Philippine Islands. What interest there was in foreign affairs was now directed toward Europe. Even World War I did not produce a ripple of interest in the Philippine Islands. It was only with the appointment of a new Governor General, Leonard B. Wood, under the administration of President Harding, that interest in the Philippines was again revived. We now found that not only had Filipinization of the insular government transpired but that the Filipino government in the Islands had taken over railroads, major utilities, banks, and large businesses.

We became interested in this laboratory experiment of government in business. The political struggle that ensued between Governor Wood and the Filipino leaders was prolonged. As is usual in a clash of principles there is an undercurrent of struggle between personalities espousing or contesting the principle at issue. America's interest, however, was again waning. We were again becoming more provincial in our preoccupations. The increased production in the Philippines of vegetable oils chiefly derived from the coconut, and also the rapidly expanding sugar industry, had aroused the fear of our own agricultural interests during the great business depression that followed in the wake of the war that retention of the Philippine Islands with the commercial protection of free trade between the Islands and the United States would provide more and more competition with agricultural enterprises in our own country. This competition for markets in oils and sugar was indeed a new form of sectionalism in American life. We were more and more inclined to hasten the day of Filipino independence which we had promised all along.

The inauguration of Manuel Quezon as first President of the Commonwealth of the Philippines occurred November 15, 1935. The people of the United States were proud of this fulfillment of their promise. To be sure, the Filipino independence act—the Tydings-McDuffie Act—which was signed by President Franklin D. Roosevelt March 24, 1934, provided that complete withdrawal of the United States Government should not transpire until 1946, and that during the 10-year interval the necessary political and commercial adjustments were to be made. This law provides for the establishment of Philippine independence after a 10-year transitional commonwealth government under a Filipino chief executive. The United States pledged itself to abandon military bases in the Philippines. The question of naval bases was held open. Immigration from the Islands was limited to a maximum annual quota of 50.

Reciprocal free trade relations between the United States and the Philippines have existed since 1909. The Tydings-McDuffie Act continued these relations during the 10-year transitional period except that annual quotas were set up on imports into the United States of Philippine products particularly of raw and refined sugar, coconut oil, and of abacá (Manila hemp) cordage, rope and twine.

The new constitution, drafted by a constitutional convention, provides for a single legislative chamber, the National Assembly, of 120 members chosen every 3 years, with extensive powers over the judiciary, regulation of capital and labor, utility franchises, supervision of power development, and exploitation of natural resources. The term of the president and vice president, according to a constitutional amendment, is 4 years, and the president can succeed himself.

A supreme court, comprising a chief justice and six justices appointed by the president, cannot declare a law or a treaty unconstitutional except by a two-thirds vote. Freedom of the press and religion and right of assembly are guaranteed in the bill of rights.

Women, to whom the suffrage on equal terms with men was granted by the legislature, while they voted in large numbers for the adoption of the constitution, were disfranchised by it until 300,000 of them voted for women suffrage in a specially called plebiscite. English and Spanish remain the official languages.

The United States trade with the Philippine Islands has always been unfavorable inasmuch as American demand for Philippine products has exceeded Philippine purchases in the United States. It was thought that free trade between the two countries would equalize trade balances although America has gradually become the chief market for Philippine products including gold, in which the Philippine Islands now rank fifth among world producers. The Islands continued to purchase less from us than they sold to us. Japan in recent years has practically monopolized the sale of textiles in the Islands. Then the Philippines have for more than a century been compelled to purchase rice in Rangoon and other Oriental ports since the Philippines, like other tropical countries that produce export crops other than foodstuffs, must import food, particularly breadstuffs.

The improvement in economic life of the Filipino people as a whole is that which is usually witnessed when a comparatively dense population is in transition from a handicraft and agricultural to an industrial economy. It is true that the mainstay of Filipino economic life remains the cultivation of land in export crops of sugar, coconuts, tobacco, and fiber, chiefly abacá hemp for rope making, but economic improvements in the form of road construction, bridges, and improvement of transportation generally, including the charting of coastal waters and the maintenance of lighthouses, has completely modernized the economic outlook of the leading agricultural areas. The improvement of the port of Manila alone is a great achievement in the development of shipping. The construction of the huge breakwater and of several large docks so that the largest ocean-going vessels may unload passengers and cargo under modern conditions is in line with the maintenance of improved forms of transportation and communication throughout the entire island group. A degree of modernization in Filipino economic life has been brought to pass.

2

THE PHILIPPINE ISLANDS AND INDONESIA

Indonesia is a geographical term used to include all the islands off the southeast coast of Asia as far east as New Guiana. The most important of the Indonesian islands—Borneo, Java, Sumatra, Celebes, and the Philippine Islands—have been occupied perhaps since the beginning of man's estate as a cultural being. The Polynesians, occupying certain of the islands of the Pacific far to the east, no doubt passed through the southernmost of these islands during their period of dispersal or migration from the Asiatic continent. Perhaps, too, the Melanesians of New Guinea and other dark-skinned races also passed through these Indonesian islands before they reached their home in Oceanic island groups and in Australia. The Indonesians belong to yet another or to several other early migratory groups from southeastern Asia. They, therefore, form a southern Mongolian stock of widely varied origin, with certain negroid minorities or ethnic islands and pockets widely dispersed throughout the larger islands.

One usually refers to the Malay as the most representative of the Indonesian peoples. He is, however, a modern arrival. He possesses much more initiative than the earlier Indonesian immigrant peoples. He is a great trader and possesses a certain political sense which enabled him to form large political organizations that in a short time penetrated but did not entirely control all of Indonesia.

No region of the earth is so rich in ethnic types, so articulated and so hybridized as Indonesia.

The island formation of Indonesia is a continuation of the mountain chains of southeastern Asia, and lies altogether in the tropical zone between latitude 10° S. and approximately 20° N. of the Equator with the exception of Formosa, which extends well into the North Temperate Zone. The four large Sunda islands—Sumatra, Java, Borneo, and Celebes—and a large number of other smaller islands are the surviving portions of a primitive, partially submerged continental land mass, the sunken southeast end of "farther India." It lies altogether within the area of the monsoons—mighty downpourings more or less evenly distributed throughout the year.

Indonesia lies at the boundary of southeastern Asia, facing on the one hand Micronesia, the small island archipelago east of the Philippines; on another, Melanesia; and on still another, New Guinea, the northern barrier to Australia far to the southeast. It fronts southeastern Asia as a compact insular land mass, but has anciently sent out an ethnic tentacle as far west as the island of Madagascar on the southeastern coast of Africa.

The mountains of farther India and Burma pass out of the interior of Asia and open up like the leaves of a fan toward the south and southeast. Their altitude becomes gradually lower until the island world of Indonesia appears as the opened, much-bisected, and flattened end of the Indo-Chinese mountain system. The more these systems open up, the more space remains for the inserted valleys. In the moist mountain altitudes there begin numerous and magnificent rivers with broad valleys, rivers rich in sediment terminating in mighty alluvial deltas. To them is owed the consolidation of distinct ethnic stocks and the foundation of states. As in India, there is observed the contrast in close juxtaposition of fruit-ful, extensive plains, suitable for development of culture, and abrupt, high mountain chains, the refuge place of more primitive peoples. The general direction of mountain chains and river valleys is north and south; obviously, the most important waves of migration were in similar direction toward the south.

The waters of the various passages separating Borneo and the Sunda islands of Java and Sumatra from the mainland of Asia at the southern portion of the Malay peninsula are so shallow that a rise of a mere 150 feet of the ocean bottom would again unite all of them, as in the geologic past they were united, with the Asiatic mainland. Similarly, if the ocean bottom were to rise only half as much, the island of Halmahera, which forms the southeastern continuation of the Philippine archipelago, would be united with the great island of New Guinea.

CONTINENTAL AFFILIATIONS

Indonesia is divided by geologists and biologists into two great halves— a western and an eastern. The former constitutes a more or less sub-merged part of the continent of Asia; the eastern half is closely linked with Australia, and at one time formed a continuous land mass with New Guinea and that continent. In the great southern chain of Indonesian islands, the Dutch East Indies, the dividing line between these two con-tinental areas as established by Wallace passes through the narrow but deep channel which separates the islands of Bali and Lombok and then continues northward through the Straits of Macassar with the great islands of Sumatra, Java, and Borneo possessing Asiatic affiliations; and Celebes, the Moluccas, and New Guinea are the principal islands that link up with Australia.

The animal life of the two divisions is markedly distinct. In the west, such well-known forms of the Asiatic mainland as the elephant, rhinoceros, tapir, tiger, and orangutan are found; in the east, marsupials, notably the kangaroo, the flightless cassowary, and birds of paradise are characteristic.

The fact that the southeastern Asiatic mammals such as the orangutan, the elephant, the tapir, and the tiger are also found on Sumatra and Borneo appears to indicate that the shallow waters separating these two great islands were at one time in the geologic past connected by a land bridge. A further observation that these animals did not reach the Philippines indicates that the land bridge between Borneo and the Philippine island, Palawan, did not exist in Quaternary times. Nevertheless, the fauna and flora of the Philippines contain a large number of Asiatic forms even though the great Asiatic mammals did not extend their range beyond Borneo. A striking contrast in biological life forms is noted in the islands beyond Halmahera, the easterly extension of the Philippine cordillera, on the great islands of New Guinea and the still greater continental mass of Australia on the south, where appears a fauna, unknown in the Philippines and on its neighboring islands, characterized by Asiatic mammalian life forms. The marsupial mammals, such as the kangaroo and the duck-billed, egg-laying mammal, the platypus of Australia, the bird of paradise, with its gorgeous plumage on the island of New Guinea, and the cassowary, the great bird that is incapable of flight, are sufficiently striking examples to point out the faunal difference that exists between these land areas and the Philippines.

In the Philippines biological affiliations are primarily with Asiatic continental life forms. Thus even in the absence of the larger mammals, all the islands forming the archipelago reveal many identical or affiliated plant forms and animal types. The biological and geological line separating plant and animal forms of the Philippine archipelago from New Guinea to the southeast is much more striking. More specifically, however, it may be stated that the Philippines, together with the Moluccas, Celebes, and other smaller intervening islands, shared a transitional position with regard to fauna and flora which was related to neither of the continental areas—Australia to the southeast and Asia on the west. Extending 1,150 miles from north to south and 682 miles from east to west, the Philippine archipelago is of such scope as to lead one to expect within this area many affiliations of plant and animal life.

RACIAL ANCESTRY OF THE FILIPINO

In racial characteristics, a similar division exists between the peoples occupying the western and the eastern island groups of Indonesia. The western islands, of which the peoples of the Philippines are typical, are in the main inhabited by brown, straight-haired peoples, the erroneously so-called Malay race of the older books. Their primary relationships are unquestionably Mongoloid and therefore Asiatic. In the eastern half of the Dutch East Indies and also in the eastern Philippines, black, broad-nosed, and wavy- or curly-haired people predominate—in fact, constitute the sole native type east of the axial cordillera in northeastern Luzon. Farther east, far beyond the Philippine Islands and far out into the Pacific lies Melanesia, the region of "black islanders." These people, while not identical with the Negrito of the Philippines, are very similar to them.

The eastward advance of the brown Mongoloid Indonesians has carried them a short distance beyond the channel between the islands of Lombok and Bali that separate the two continental areas. Celebes and parts of the Moluccas, although in the Australian half of the Indies, are occupied racially primarily by Indonesians. It is obvious, then, that the human distribution has come to deviate somewhat from the range and continental affiliations of animals and plants and the underlying geological formations. The line of demarkation between the brown and black peoples extending north from Australia bends far to the east almost to the Kei and Aru Islands which it passes on the west in a sigmoid curve extending northwest between Ceram Island and the outlying islets off the western tip of the subcontinental island of New Guinea. The remarkable tenacity of the earlier black Negrito type is observable in the northern continuation of the line which bisects the eastern Moluccas and the entire Philippine archipelago from south to north. Here we find the brown, straight-haired Indonesian Filipino living west of the line and the small-statured, kinky-haired, black Negrito—an ethnic survival—east of the line which in the Philippines follows the axial cordillera from northern Luzon to southern Mindanao. It is a striking observation, however, to note an almost unbroken demarkation line between the brown Indonesians and the black Negrito and Melanesian that closely parallels the biological line established by Weber as marking the division existing between the two insular worlds within Indonesia having biological and geological affiliations with Asia on the west and with Australia on the east.

TOPOGRAPHY, CLIMATE, AND POPULATION

The two larger Philippine islands—Luzon on the north, Mindanao on the south—contain each within its own borders variation in topography and climate. Variation in climate is accentuated by the mountain ranges traversing each of the islands in a general south-north direction and by the extensive interior valleys. The entire mountain system of the Philippines is a succession of volcanic ranges and contains at least 20 more or less active volcanoes. In Luzon the volcanoes Taal and Mayon are not as high as Mount Apo in Mindanao which reaches a height of 9,610 feet. There have been a number of eruptions within historic times, and although seriously destructive to life and vegetation in the immediate vicinity, none of the eruptions have assumed the catastrophic proportions of the outbreak of the volcano Krakatoa in Sunda Strait in 1883.

Intermittent local disturbances of the earth's surface due to earthquakes, although of common occurrence, have likewise not resulted in serious destruction to life owing to the type of construction of most of the Filipino homes, which are built primarily of bamboo and of rattan. Reinforced concrete structures in Manila have withstood all earthquakes, although masonry walls of the most substantial type, as the massive city walls and great churches within the walled city, have all been seriously damaged or entirely destroyed by earthquakes.

Typhoons, which are very destructive to life and property, are limited to a belt which includes only the northern and the central islands. Mindanao and the Jolo archipelago are entirely free from typhoons and enjoy a climate characteristic of the equatorial belt. The temperatures throughout the islands vary according to local conditions and distances from the seacoast, although the entire archipelago has but little variation throughout the year. A local variation from the relatively high humidity occurs in western Luzon during the autumn and winter dry season. The small Batanes group north of Luzon almost touches the northern limits of the Tropics and has a correspondingly cooler climate. The elevated areas of north-central Luzon, also the area surrounding Lake Lanao in north-central Mindanao have a mountain climate with cool nights. In the province of Benguet in the vicinity of Baguio, winter frosts are not uncommon. Here bamboo thickets are replaced by pine forests, and native construction of houses with pine wood flooring and walls is characteristic. In the province of Benguet and on the Baguio plateau, at an altitude of 4,700 feet, frosts occur in December and January, while on the higher peaks of northern Luzon ice forms on water. Wet snow storms are not uncommon on the higher peaks of northern Luzon during the winter months.

The distribution of native population does not follow the lines of natural topography. Some of the most densely populated areas in northern Luzon are the most mountainous. In the mountain province the Ifugao, Bontoc, Kalinga, and Nabaloi have attained a population density of more than 150 per square mile—almost that of an industrial area in the United States—while some lowland peoples occupying valley land are widely dispersed. Another mountain stock, the Apayao, occupying a mountainous area in extreme northwestern Luzon, larger than that of the Ifugao, has a lower occupational density. Then, in the river valleys much of the land suitable for use in crop production is not at all occupied, but overgrown with dense cogon grass which is of use for grazing purposes only when it is young, but coarse and useless when it is mature. In Mindanao with topographic conditions roughly comparable to those of Luzon and a land area of equal proportion, similarly divided between lowland river valleys and mountainous uplands, we find that the numerous ethnic groups such as the pagan Bagobo, Manobo, Bukidnon, and others have only a fraction of the population maintained by the pagan ethnic groups of the narrow mountain valleys of northern Luzon. The explanation lies not in the topography itself, nor in climatic conditions which are roughly similar throughout the archipelago with alternating periods of rainfall and drought, but in the prevailing type of land utilization, and in the methods used in rice production, the staple food. Those pagan groups cultivating rice by means of irrigation, as in the upland mountainous regions of north-central Luzon, developed dense population because of the necessity for maintaining communal agriculture and the maintenance of the huge irrigation system, while those planting upland rice on unirrigated soil possess less need for communal control of agricultural procedures and may be widely dispersed.

To the Filipino peoples, long inured to the constant heat and humidity found throughout the entire archipelago, climatic conditions within the area occupied are perhaps normal. Whether the intense humidity and heat, which at times become almost unbearable to the individual reared in a temperate environment, have in the long run and independent of other contributory factors retarded the development of the Filipino is a purely hypothetical problem. To him, this climate is normal and not extreme. With the exception of a few favored areas, however, namely, the uplands of north-central Luzon where the summer capitol, Baguio, was early established by the American insular government, and the great upland plateau of northern Mindanao in the vicinity of Lake Lanao, now occupied by large cattle ranches, the climate of the Philippines is definitely obnoxious to many occupational classes of the temperate zone. The Philippine Islands constitute no favorable exception to tropical climate generally.

There are, nevertheless, two definitely distinct types of climate in the Philippines roughly localized in the eastern and western portions of the archipelago, on the opposite sides of the main mountain axis. The entire area east of the main cordillera, particularly from central Luzon southward, has no dry season and rainfall is continuous throughout the year, whereas in the extreme western portion of the archipelago, particularly in the Visayan Islands and in Luzon, the winter is definitely a dry season. This variation in rainfall, of course, is due to seasonal variation in prevailing winds. From November to June the northeast trade wind prevails, and consequently the east coasts have a heavy rainfall, while most of the rest of the archipelago, being protected by the east coast ranges, is comparatively dry. During the remaining four months the southwest summer monsoon prevails producing a rainy season over most of the archipelago, while the east coasts are comparatively dry.

Deforested and eroded hills and mountains are characteristic of many upland regions of Luzon and the Visayas, where the gradual substitution of grasslands for forest may be ascribed to the firing of clearings which are characteristic of the caiñgining or "hoe culture" where clearings are abandoned to encroaching grasses and weeds after 1 or 2 years. The dense agricultural population of the lowland river valleys in central Luzon has eliminated primary forests where extensive areas are permanently occupied in irrigated rice culture. Then, too, the long dry winter season tends to retard forest growth in the greater portion of Luzon west of the main cordillera where immense areas are overgrown with the tall, coarse, commercially worthless cogon grass, while in Mindanao, which is more exposed to the easterly rain-bearing monsoon winds throughout the year, the forest growth both primary and secondary is intense, covering practically the entire island with a dense mass of vegetation. This fact may in part explain the limited development of agriculture and the low population density among the pagan tribes of eastern and central Mindanao who do not possess the traction plow and are consequently unable to cope with encroaching tough root grasses.

As in other portions of the world, the increase in population in the Philippine Islands during the past three centuries has been great. An estimated population of 500,000 at the time of the Spanish conquest is contrasted with the population total of 16,356,000 established by the 1940 census. We cannot be entirely certain that this increase can be attributed to the same causes that have accounted for the increase in population elsewhere throughout the world, namely, an increased food supply resulting from development of trade, and the consequent security due to suppression of local intervillage warfare. Certainly we may not assume that improved sanitation and medical attention apply to the agricultural Philippines in the same manner that these factors would operate

PLATE 5

1. PANDANUS PALMS, LAGUNA PROVINCE. LUZON

The broad leaf of the pandanus palm, *Pandanus utilissimus,* is universally put to innumerable uses in the arts, as in the weaving of hats, baskets, mats, and generally as a substitute for coarse fabrics.

2. THE RATTAN PALM, BALIUAG. BULACAN PROVINCE. LUZON

The rattan palm, *Calamus mollis,* ranks next to bamboo in importance as an economic plant. In the hands of the Filipino it replaces practically all other tying and binding materials requiring flexibility, strength, and durability.

PLATE 6

2. COOKING RICE IN A CUT STEM OF GREEN BAMBOO

A Tagalog of Rizal Province, Luzon, is illustrating the general practice of improvising a cooking utensil from a green bamboo stem. The rice is cooked long before the bamboo begins to char.

1. A BAMBOO-STEM WATER BUCKET, PROVINCE OF ILOCOS NORTE, LUZON

The Ilocano school boy climbing a bamboo stile is carrying water in a cut section of bamboo stem from which all nodal septums except the one at the bottom have been removed. Containers of this type are in general use.

1. A TAGALOG FARMER PLOWING, ANTIPOLO, LUZON

The use of the traction plow in irrigated rice culture depends on the steadfast qualities of the water buffalo or carabao.

2. HARVESTING RICE WITH SICKLES, RIZAL PROVINCE, LUZON

Irrigated rice ripens after the close of the rainy season. Although the fields are now dry, the grain is cut with a simple hand sickle.

1. BONTOC-IGOROT WOMEN TRANSPLANTING RICE, NORTHERN LUZON

The methods used by the Bontoc and Ifugao of the mountain province in cultivating irrigated rice are essentially similar to lowland practices although their fields are too small to use a carabao-drawn plow.

2. TERRACED RICE FIELDS OF THE IFUGAO, BANAUE, NORTHERN LUZON

in a large city in a temperate zone. The influence of Spanish governmental control over piracy, head hunting, and local feuding may be assigned as leading factors in the truly great increase in the Island population.

HEALTH AND SANITATION

The coming of American sanitary control, and the further suppression of feudal life in the eight districts of the mountain province of northern Luzon, and of killing and slaving raids by the Moro in the southern Philippines have further tended to increase the ratio of population growth. The natural causes formerly decimating native Filipino population such as periodic outbreaks of cholera in the nineteenth century, notably in 1820, 1862, 1882, and 1889, bubonic plague, smallpox, and other diseases of civilization have been practically eliminated from Philippine life through use of serum and mass vaccination. The pock-marked faces of the older adult population are not observable among the young. Cholera epidemics have been practically eliminated through the use of serum.

Victor Heiser, in his book "An American Doctor's Odyssey," refers to old-time Manila as a cesspool of disease. During a cholera epidemic the morgue was piled high with the victims. Rats overran the city. Lepers and the insane throughout the archipelago were not given special treatment but remained either prisoners in their own homes or went at large. The control of malaria and the related dengue fever, however, can never be complete in tropical countries with our existing knowledge and equipment for combating mosquitoes. Such progress as was made in the control of plague, cholera, and smallpox epidemics and in the segregation of the leper and the insane cannot be reported for malaria and intestinal fungus.

In public health the achievement of the American colonial administration in the Philippine Islands has been remarkably successful. The early removal of all lepers from other parts of the Islands to a leper colony established on the Island of Culion has eliminated all danger of the spread of leprosy. The establishment of hospitals in many of the larger towns and a medical school and nurses' training school in Manila have facilitated the development of the progress of public health. The presence of an artesian basin in the densely populated central Luzon plain has made possible the procurement of pure drinking water through the sinking of hundreds of artesian wells. Thus the spread of diseases induced by the drinking of contaminated water has to a large extent ceased. Manila has become one of the cleanest cities in the Far East.

When the medical corps accompanying the first American expedition surveyed health conditions in the city of Manila they found an infant mortality rate of approximately 80 per 100. Four out of five babies died. In 1940 the death rate was 60 per 1,000—14 out of 15 babies lived. Throughout the archipelago where supervision and hospitalization are possible the infant mortality rate is much less than formerly and approaches that of the city of Manila. The Filipino family, including all the *parientes*, is a vital institution in Indonesian society.

FOREIGN NATIONALS

An interesting comparison in the population of the two larger islands—Luzon and Mindanao—reveals a population ratio of 4:1 in favor of the culturally more advanced Luzon. This is in part due to the development of the great trade city, Manila, with its population of 623,362. The foreign population of the Islands, according to the 1940 census, reached a total of 166,977 and included 117,461 Chinese, 29,272 Japanese, and 8,739 Americans, exclusive of the military and naval personnel and their families. Of the foreign population scattered throughout the Islands, a great majority lives in Manila and other large trading centers. Many of the Chinese are married to native women and have become members of the Catholic church. They have, to a great extent, therefore, become amalgamated into the ethnic group where they reside. While the Chinese are primarily tradesmen, many of the Japanese are farmers, craftsmen, and fishermen. They do not intermarry with the population but bring their entire families with them.

Numerous Asiatic immigrant groups may be distinguished. Among the more recent are many Syrians and Turks who are engaged in commercial and professional occupations. The Spanish colony in Manila remains a numerous, close-knitted group characterized by its conservatism and old-established position, and for its intense sponsorship of the independence movement. The Spanish have been particularly successful in the tobacco industry and in shipping. Other minor groups of Europeans include English, Swiss, French, Italian, Dutch, Belgian, German, and the Roumanian Jew. The purely commercial activities of the Islands are primarily in the hands of the comparatively small foreign-born element.

The Philippines have enjoyed accretions of population by way of immigration from the Asiatic mainland and the great semicontinental islands of the East Indies lying to the south, and have received many contributions of material culture as well. The history of race mixture in the Philippine Islands does not extend beyond their discovery to the Spanish by Magellan in 1521, but this does not preclude a comparison of the various layers or strata of culture which have remained to the present day. Chinese intermarriage with the Tagalog and other lowland stocks has produced a large class of Chinese mestizos, mostly in the cities. The influence of the Spanish physical type is almost everywhere apparent. The Spanish were in possession of the most populous and the richest territory for more than 300 years, and through their intermarriage with native women, an appreciable segment of the Christian population reveals traces of Spanish blood. Spanish influence constituted the veneer of Filipino physical types while the older Indonesian and Malay strata lay clearly indicated underneath the striking features of the Spanish mestizos. The Spanish army, always small, was built up for the most part with levies of soldiers from Peru and Mexico. The number of Peninsular Spanish in the Islands never exceeded more than a few thousand men.

THE SPANISH EXPERIMENT IN GLOBAL GEOGRAPHY

Ferdinand Magellan first reached the eastern Philippine island of Samar, March 16, 1521. We have the narrative of his voyage of discovery from Antonio Pigafetta who accompanied the expedition to the Philippines and was fortunate enough to be aboard the one ship, the *Victoria,* that returned out of the five that had departed from Seville. Pigafetta refers to the interisland trade in existence between the Malays of Brunei in Borneo, Cagayan in western Mindanao, and the Visayan island of Leyte. He observed and tells about the native cultivation of rice, and refers to the presence of coconuts, oranges, bananas, breadfruit, and ginger. Another observation, if true, is startling, namely, his remark that he observed the cultivation of maize on the small island of Limasaua near the south end of the island of Leyte. Since maize or Indian corn first became known to the Portuguese through the Spanish, who for the first time saw it growing in the West Indies in 1492, its presence in the Philippine Islands, where it was not indigenous, a scant 30 years later is remarkable.

Magellan, anxious to obtain adequate food supplies for his crew, extended his explorations. Passing the island of Bohol he arrived at Cebu, at that time a native town of several thousand inhabitants. Here further evidence of interisland trade was noted in the presence of a Siamese junk.

The ability of the Filipino as a trader in 1521 is evidenced by the observation of Pigafetta that Cebu merchants were in possession of balance scales, weights and measures, and that they had a good knowledge of the relative value of commodities.

It might be noted that the desire to Christianize the populations of newly discovered lands fired the enthusiasm of the Spanish explorer as much as it does our own great missionary societies. The extent to which Magellan succeeded during his brief stay on the island of Cebu in "Christianizing" the native population is difficult to understand. However, Pigafetta refers to the *dato* of Cebu as having become a Christian. The observance of mass by the Spaniards must have made a strong emotional appeal. Eight hundred Filipinos, including Humabom their chief or *dato*, were baptized. Magellan was killed soon afterward while assisting the "Christianized" Cebuans in a fight with the natives of the nearby island of Mactan.

Still searching for the Moluccas, the expedition passed by a small number of islands of the Cagayan Sulu group, the island of Palawan where was observed with interest the native sport of cock fighting, and landed finally at Brunei, a strong Mohammedan town on the northwest coast of the island of Borneo. Pigafetta states that Brunei consisted of two sections: one, that of the native Dyak Malay population, the other, that of the Mohammedan Malay who were in possession of gunpowder and numerous brass cannon. The expedition then sailed to Mindanao, where native pearl fishing excited their interest. Requiring guides, they resorted to the customary Spanish procedure of obtaining prisoners and interpreters. Finally the island of Tidor, one of the Molucca Islands, 250 miles south of Mindanao, was reached. A trade agreement and form of treaty was arranged with the *rajas*, Almanzar, of the island of Tidor, and Yusef (Joseph) of the much larger island of Gilolo (Halmahera). At last it was possible to get down to the real purpose of the expedition, namely, trade. A trading post was established, and it was hoped that these islands could be held against the Portuguese. The Spaniards exchanged cloth for a rich cargo of cloves, sandalwood, ginger, cinnamon, and gold. It was decided to send one ship, the *Victoria*, to Spain under the command of Juan Sebastian Elcano by way of the Cape of Good Hope following the established Portuguese route. The other remaining ship out of the original five was to return to the Spanish colonies in America. This latter ship was never heard from again, while the *Victoria* sailed first to Timor, another small island of the Moluccas, and then through the Indian Ocean, around the southern end of Africa, finally reaching the Portuguese Cape Verde Islands where Elcano anchored, hoping to obtain supplies, thinking that the Portuguese would not suspect them so far away from the Moluccas. The Portuguese governor, however, gave orders for the seizure of the *Victoria* and Elcano raised sail, arriving at San Lucar, Spain, September 6, 1522, with 18 men left out of the original company of 234. Spain welcomed the return of the expedition. Elcano was given the significant coat-of-arms showing the clove, cinnamon, and the nutmeg plant, also a globe with the inscription, "Primus circumdedisti me."

The voyage, designed to appropriate for the Spanish the trade with the East Indies already established by the Portuguese, actually led to the discovery of the Philippine Islands to the western world. It incidentally brought about the first circumnavigation of the globe and set in motion the cultural forces that have operated from that time on to isolate the peoples of the Philippines from earlier cultural affiliations and from physically related populations in Indonesia. At the same time it magnified the importance of Manila as the commercial center of the Far East, and the entrepôt through which the kingdoms of eastern Asia exchanged their wares. Here came great fleets of junks from China laden with stores. Morga, writing in 1609, fills nearly two pages with an enumeration of their merchandise, which included all manner of silks, brocades, furniture, pearls and gems, fruits, nuts, tame buffalo, geese, horses and mules, all kinds of animals, "even to birds in cages, some of which talk and others sing, and which they make perform a thousand tricks; there are innumerable other gewgaws and knickknacks, which among Spaniards are in much esteem."

Each year a fleet of 30 to 40 Chinese junks sailed with the new moon in March. The voyage across the China Sea, rough with the monsoons, occupied 15 or 20 days, and the fleet returned at the end of May or the beginning of June. Between October and March there came each year Japanese ships from Nagasaki which brought wheat, silks, objects of art, and weapons, and took away from Manila the raw silk of China, gold, deer horns, woods, honey, wax, palm wine and wine of Castile.

From Malacca and India came fleets of the Portuguese subjects of Spain, with spices, slaves, Negroes, and Kafirs, and the rich productions of Bengal, India, Persia, and Turkey. From Borneo, too, came the smaller craft of the Malays, who from their boats sold the fine palm mats, the best of which still come from Cagayan Sulu and Borneo, slaves, sago, water pots, and glazed earthenware, black and fine. From Siam and Cambodia also, but less often, there came trading ships. Manila had become a great emporium for all the countries of the East.

The subject of the early trade routes of Spanish galleons in the Pacific is an interesting study. The route of these great vessels which were engaged in the Philippine trade on leaving Manila extended northeastward from Luzon approximately to the 42d degree of latitude. The westerly winds prevailing in this latitude enabled the galleon to sail nearly straight eastward across the Pacific to Cape Mendocino in northern California. Thence, the galleon's course laid down the western coast of North America nearly 3,000 miles to the port of Acapulco on the west coast of Mexico and 800 miles south of Cape San Lucas at the southern end of Lower California.

The commerce between the Philippines, and Mexico and Spain, though it was of vast importance, was soon limited by action of the crown. It was a commerce which apparently admitted of infinite expansion, but the shortsighted merchants and manufacturers of the Peninsula clamored against its development, and it was subjected to the severest limitations. Four galleons were at first maintained for this trade, which were dispatched two at a time in successive years from Manila to the port of Acapulco, Mexico. These galleons were great ships of 600 and 800 tons apiece. They went "very strong with soldiers," and they carried the annual mail, reenforcements, and supplies of Mexican silver for trade with China, which has remained the commercial currency of the East almost to the present day. Later the number of galleons was reduced to one.

The solitary galleon was freighted with the pick of all the rich stores that came to Manila. The profits were enormous—600 and 800 percent. Biscaino wrote that with 200 ducats invested in Spanish wares and some Flemish commodities, he made 1,400 ducats; but, he added, in 1588 he lost a ship—robbed and burned by Englishmen.

For generations these galleons were probably the most tempting and romantic prizes that ever aroused the cupidity of a privateer. In 1596 the galleon *San Felipe* was lost with a valuable cargo of spice, ivory, amber, perfume, Chinese porcelain, silk and other fabrics on the coast of Japan. In 1604 the *San Antonio* with 300 people aboard was lost at sea. Other galleons fell into the hands of the Dutch and British. A few years before Mexico gained her independence from Spain the galleon trade was discontinued.

CHINESE TRADERS

The Spanish found the presence of Chinese traders in Manila an absolute essential to their existence. The scarcity of local food supplies not only attests to the sparse native population of the Philippine Islands at the time of the first Spanish settlements, but made the importation of rice and other foodstuffs from China necessary. In the galleon trade with New Spain (Mexico) which later developed, the Spanish found that a cargo of goods imported originally from China to Manila where it was transshipped to the official cargo of the galleon produced greater profits than did the export of such things as could be obtained locally in the Philippines. On the other hand, the Chinese were eager to trade with the Spanish in order to obtain the Mexican pesos and Spanish gold.

Luzon was known to the Chinese long before the Spanish conquest. The native Indonesian name "Luzong" appeared in Chinese texts as "Lü-Sung." Like the Japanese, the Chinese applied this term to the entire archipelago although the Chinese meant the City of Manila in most instances when reference was made to the name Lü-Sung. This term appears in "Ming Shih," the Chinese Annals of the Ming Dynasty, along with many other references to the Philippines generally. According to these Annals, a delegation from Luzon actually arrived in China with gifts as early as the year 1372. The Chinese emperor exchanged gifts with the embassy in the form of silk and cloth of gold. There is no evidence that the Chinese had settlements or colonies in the Philippine Islands previous to the Spanish conquest. Nevertheless, trading vessels came to the Islands with the fall monsoon. A Chinese author, Chao Ju-Kua, in 1205, in describing the maritime commerce of the Chinese people, devoted one chapter of his work to the trade with the Philippines to which he refers as "Mayi," presumably Manila. The Filipinos traded cotton goods, beeswax, coconuts, and woven palm leaf mats for Chinese silk parasols, porcelains, and rattan baskets. Manila is described in this Chinese document as containing a thousand families living along the banks of a very winding stream. This Chinese author also refers to an ancient Philippine cotton costume resembling the sarong—the garment we no longer associate with westernized Philippine peoples. The author naïvely explains that the captain of the Chinese junk, when entering the port of Manila, presented the *datos* with white umbrellas. This was a form of tribute levied preliminary to obtaining the good will of local chieftains. The products of the country are described as yellow beeswax, cotton, pearls, shells, areca nuts, abacá, and piña cloth. The Chinese exported porcelain, objects of lead and iron, including iron cooking pans and needles, and glass beads in variegated colors.

Chao Ju-Kua in this narrative makes probably what is the first mention of the Negritos. He makes this reference:

In the interior of the valleys lives a race called "Haitan" (Aeta). They are of low stature, have round eyes of a yellow color, curly hair, and their teeth are easily seen between their lips. They build their nests in the tree tops and in each nest lives a family, which only consists of from three to five persons. They travel about in the densest thickets of the forests, and without being seen themselves, shoot their arrows at the passers by; for this reason they are much feared. If the trader throws them a small porcelain bowl they will stoop down to catch it and then run away with it shouting joyfully.

Another reference to the Philippines taken from the Annals of the Ming Shih is to the Pangasinan people who originally occupied much of the area of the valley of central Luzon and of the northwest coast of Luzon. The Pangasinan must have been an energetic and enterprising people for this reference in the Ming Shih speaks of an embassy from them to China in 1406 as presenting some horses to the Chinese emperor, Yung-Lo. It is generally understood that the Filipinos, particularly in Jolo and in Mindanao, did have horses before the arrival of the Spaniard. The emperor very graciously gave the Pangasinan delegation paper money in return, as well as bolts of silk. The Chinese emperor, Yung-Lo, appears to have sent an officer to Luzon during the previous year, namely in 1405, who was to remain as the governor of that island. This interesting detail in the narrative of the Annals of the Ming Dynasty indicates that the first protectorate over the Philippines was Chinese. This statement gains probability when it is remembered that the Ming emperors were aggressive and inclined to enlarge the territory over which they ruled.

The first contact between the Spaniards and Chinese was in 1571 in Mindoro. The Chinese, however, had been established in Luzon before that time in considerable numbers. It is mentioned in the Ming Shih, that "Formerly the people of Fukien lived there because the place was conveniently near." The many conflicts with the Chinese colonies established in Manila from time to time and their bloody extinction by the Spanish and Filipinos form a part of narrative history and do not in themselves contribute to a study of the cultural development of the people of the Philippines.

POT HUNTERS FROM CIPANGO

The Japanese had long been interested in exploring the island of Luzon to obtain porcelain and stoneware jars of ancient Sung and Ming Chinese dynastic origin. These ceramic wares were highly prized by the Filipinos who in later years had lost all remembrance of their previous history. This search for Chinese burial jars by Japanese pot hunters in the Philippine Islands represents a peculiar phase of Japanese effort which is related neither to commerce nor to political aggression. In the old Chinese narrative of Chao Ju-Kua there is mention of the sporadic arrival of the individual Japanese traveler in Luzon whose interest was directed almost entirely to the recovery and removal to Japan of some of these rare old Chinese jars around which the Filipinos, ignorant of their provenience, have in recent centuries built up a great amount of superstitious folklore. The Japanese travelers appear, however, to have been interested in these jars merely as art collectors, perhaps because of their rare beauty of form, or most likely as types of ceramic wares suitable for reproduction in Japanese pottery kilns.

Antonio de Morga, however, relates of a different type of Japanese interest in the Philippines which appears as an ominous forerunner of later-day aggression. The powerful Shogun Hideyoshi in 1592 had demanded of the Spanish governor, Dasmariñas, the payment of a specified amount of tribute and threatened to attack and occupy Manila if the tribute demanded was not forthcoming. The general attitude of the Japanese toward the Spanish, however, appears to have been peaceful.

On page 45 of his study of "Chinese Pottery in the Philippines," Fay-Cooper Cole expressed the view that "we are bound to presume either that the celadons hunted by the Japanese on the Philippines were different from those imported from China, or that the Chinese imports did not suffice to fill the demand, and that the commercial opportunities afforded on the Philippines must have had a special attraction for them." This may indeed be inferred from the political events of the time. Hideyoshi's military expedition to Korea in 1597 was a blow directed against China. During the rule of the Ming Dynasty (1368-1643), commercial relations between China and Japan were crippled; Japanese corsairs pillaged the coasts of southern China, and fear of them led to the exclusion of Japanese trading vessels except those admitted on special passports, and but few Chinese junks stealthily made for Japan. Only the advance of the Manchu Dynasty brought about a change in these conditions, and after the Dutch had lost possession of Formosa (1662), China's trade with Japan began to flourish. While Hideyoshi, owing to the high ambitions of his politics, observed a hostile attitude toward China, he cast his eyes Philippineward. In 1592 he dispatched a message to the Spanish governor, Gomez Perez Dasmariñas, demanding the recognition of his supremacy; otherwise he would enforce it by an invasion and devastation of the Islands. The frightened governor, not prepared for such an attack nor willing to lose the profitable trade relations with Japan, sent an embassy under the leadership of a Dominican to the Taikō to whom he offered a treaty of amity. Hideyoshi promised to desist from military action, on payment of a yearly tribute. In 1593 the conditions of this treaty were stipulated, according to which the Japanese promised to dispatch annually to Manila ships freighted with provisions, to stop piracy, and to grant passports to Spanish captains for the safety of their ships.

3

CULTURAL INFLUENCES FROM INDIA

The influence of the Mohammedan religion and of Islamic culture on the native population of the Philippines was not deep. Improvements were introduced in the manufacture of weapons, notably of such hand weapons as had to do with representations of rank as the kris and the barong. The material culture of the population, however, was not affected in a general way. It is another influence emanating from India that penetrated the entire field of material culture. A large body of Sanskrit words was introduced along with a system of writing similar to that brought from India to other Malayan islands and to southeastern Asia, notably Cambodia, Assam, and the Malay Peninsula. The art of metal working, as well as decorative motifs based on the lotus flower and other Hindu cult representations, are characteristic of influences from India. We do not find in the Philippines remains of Hindu temples such as are found in the Buddhist center at Palembang, Sumatra, or the Brahmanist temple remains at Madjapahit in Java. Nevertheless, through trade and sporadic immigration, cultural influences penetrated the Philippines for a period perhaps extending more than 2,000 years.

Perhaps most of the ideas were indirectly introduced by way of the neighboring island of Borneo and the more strongly Hinduized Java. Borneo had previously received many settlements of Hinduized Malays probably from Madjapahit in Java. Still later, groups of Mohammedan Malays, as the Bugin from the island of Celebes, founded settlements in Borneo. Chinese also arrived to work gold deposits and to mine precious stones which they found there. Consequently, for centuries the native population of portions of the island of Borneo was under the influence of foreign civilizations or at least was in contact with cultures of a higher order than its own.

One immigrant group, the Kayan, is cited by Hose and McDougall as arriving in Borneo about the beginning of the fourteenth century. These Malays landed near Sikudana and spread throughout central Borneo. The Dyaks of the interior were doubtless soon brought in contact with either the Hindu-Malay kingdoms of the coast or the Hinduized Kayan immigrants of the interior. Hose and McDougall relate in considerable detail the methods of iron working practiced by the Kayan such as were observed and imitated by the Dyaks, who in turn became the instructors of the Sulu Moros; northern Filipino tribes may well have obtained their knowledge of iron working from a more remote Indonesian source and during a much earlier period. Archeological evidence of a pre-iron stone age in the Philippines is available, but in fragmentary form.

Because of the stronger impact of Indic cultures on these neighboring islands, its long-continued influence, even among the pagan groups throughout the Philippine archipelago, was much more penetrating than was the more recent influence of Mohammedan culture. Early Chinese writers on the Philippine Islands commented on the great numbers of bronze images (Buddhist) encountered wherever they engaged in trade. The idea of the Hindu state, such as that of Madjapahit in Java, did not extend to the Philippines. It required the Mohammedan with his caste system, including the idea of a sultanate and kingship, to disturb the tribal organization which had not been affected anywhere by cultural influences emanating from India. The structure of society remained unchanged. While the Chinese were content to remain mere traders, and left no permanent influence or impressed no Indonesian civilization, the culture emanating from India introduced ideas and knowledge of varied types, enriched the language, and radically changed fundamental religious beliefs.

An earlier religious impulse originating in India accounts for the great prehistoric culture influence reaching the Philippines. The great civilization developed in India by the Hindus is also responsible for the world religions—Braminism and Buddhism—that spread over Burma, Siam, and Java 1,500 years ago. Although temples and other great architectural ruins of Hindu civilization are not found elsewhere in the East Indies, it is clear from many sources that Hindu influence penetrated to far beyond the confines of the coast of Java. Many words in the Philippine Tagalog dialect have a Sanskrit origin, and the alphabet employed by the Filipinos at the time of their discovery by the Spanish was similar to that in use by the Hinduized Javanese. Dr. Pardo de Tavera writes "the words which Tagalog borrowed are those which signify intellectual acts, moral conceptions, emotions, superstitions, name of deities, of planets, of numerals of high number, of botany, of war and its results and consequences, and, finally, of titles and dignities, some animals, instruments of industry, and the names of money." Inasmuch as the migration of the Malay proper to the Philippine Islands in limited numbers was comparatively recent and under Mohammedan influence, it is agreed that the Sanskrit words adopted into the Tagalog and other Filipino dialects were acquired from the Hindu at a much earlier date. As the Hindus were not accustomed to making long maritime voyages, it is probable that Hindu culture was acquired piecemeal and that it passed from one island to its nearest island neighbor. There is no tribe in the Philippines, no matter how primitive and remote, in whose culture of today elements of Indian origin cannot be traced.

THE MALAY

The Malay people, not to be confused with the so-called Malay race, a term formulated by early writers solely on the prestige of the true Malay, originated according to its own tradition in western Sumatra, especially in the area of Menangkabau. As they expanded along the river courses on the east coast of the island, they had already reached a high level of culture owing to influence from India. In east Sumatra the migrating Malays came under the influence of the Javanese still more deeply permeated with Indian culture. Migrating from Palengane they founded, according to their traditional records, the town of Singapore in the year 1160. This town is supposed to have been destroyed in the year 1252 by an army of the Javanese kingdom of Madjapahit, whereupon the Malay population fled to the mainland back of the island of Singapore and founded the town of Malacca. This Malay settlement was scattered through its capture by the Portuguese in 1511. Many natives thereupon settled in various places on the Malay Peninsula. The coastal areas of Malacca Straits are the cradle of the Malay people. From this point the Malay wandered northward and eastward and to the south. They appeared as colonizers in many places, especially in Borneo. However, the settlements adhered everywhere to the coasts and river valleys. They were not a forest people like the older strata of the Indonesian peoples. They avoided mountains and forests of the interior, so that today primitive hunting and mountain peoples may be found in the Malay Peninsula and east Sumatra entirely unrelated to the true Malay.

Two circumstances facilitated the spread of the true Malay: First, the arrival of Islam in Malacca perhaps in the fourteenth century. The Malay became its missionaries, so that in many areas Mohammedans and Malays were considered one and the same. The Dyak who became a convert to Islam assumed at the same time Malay garb and costume and became a Malay. Second, the Malays who came in contact with the Portuguese in Malacca served as interpreters for them in trade with other people of Malaysia. The spread of the Portuguese conquest to the Moluccas is synonymous with the spread of Malay speech to that area. The Dutch took over the speech of the true Malay and spread it still farther as their conquests advanced.

Malay speech is rather mixed. It contains, along with many Sanskrit words, also numerous Arabic, Persian, Hindustanese, Tamil, Portuguese, Dutch, English, Spanish, and Chinese words. There are about 5,000,000 true Malays living in the East Indies. This, of course, is but a fraction of the population of Java alone. To the Europeans, because of the reasons given, the Malay assumed undue importance. Thus we have the terms

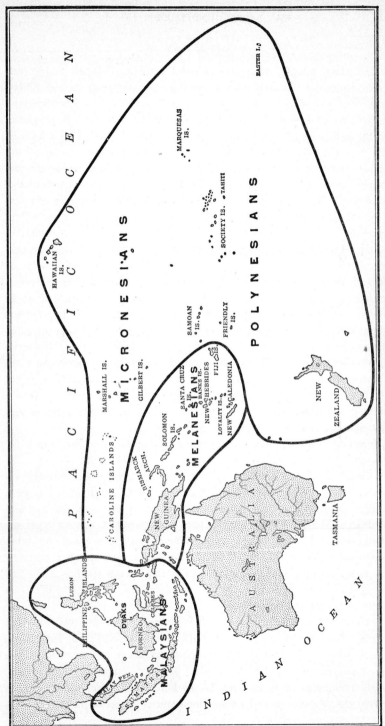

Fig. 3.—Ethnic areas in the southwest Pacific.

Malaysia, Malay Archipelago, Malay Peninsula, not to mention the erroneously so-called Malay race consisting of entire groups of Indonesians throughout the Philippines and the East Indies who have thus, through their being so designated by Europeans, become Malays. The term Indonesian, however, is likewise not satisfactory, since many scholars, following Hamy, have erroneously assumed the existence of an Indonesian subrace supposedly older than the generalized Indonesian and supposedly equipped with physical features and characteristics distinct from those of the generalized "Malayan" Indonesian race which includes the many hundreds of peoples occupying Indonesia, originally a geographical term, including the East Indies, Philippines, and Formosa. Thus the Filipino, with the exception of a fraction of the Moros living in the Sulu islands, is racially and geographically Indonesian—not Malay.

THE MORO

Arab missionaries reached Indonesia by way of India, where they had settlements on the Malabar and the Coromandel coasts. The Malays at the time of their conversion to Mohammedanism were an insignificant people living on the island of Sumatra. Under the influence of the teachings of Mohammedan missionaries and their new faith they began as early as 1250 a conquest of their own which has made the Malay the most powerful people of the East Indies. These Mohammedanized Malays defeated the Dyaks, an Indonesian tribe, of western Borneo, and established themselves on the west coast of Borneo, whence they carried on expeditions against the more primitive Indonesian tribes in the Philippines and elsewhere in the East Indies. The Spanish on their arrival in the Philippines estimated that the total native population was half a million inhabitants, of which, however, only a fraction were Mohammedanized. Outposts of the Mohammedan Moros were found established at Manila, in Luzon, and in the Visayan Islands of Mindoro, Lubang, and others.

The Mohammedan population of Mindanao and Jolo owes something certainly to this same Malay migration which founded the colony at Borneo. But the Magindanao and Illanon Moro seem to be largely descendants of primitive tribes, such as the Manobo and Tiruray, who were converted to Mohammedanism by Malay and Arab proselyters. The traditions of the Magindanao Moros ascribe their conversion to Kabunsuan, a native of Johore, the son of an Arab father and Malay mother. He came to Magindanao with a band of followers, and from him the dattos of Magindanao trace their lineage. Kabunsuan, through his Arab father, is supposed to be descended from Mohammed, and so the dattos of Magindanao to the present day proudly believe that in their veins flows the blood of the prophet. [A History of the Philippines, by David P. Barrows, p. 40.]

A strange fact is to be noted in the simultaneous warfare between Spanish and Mohammedans both in the West, in Spain and in Morocco, and in the East, in the Philippines, where the Spanish again entered upon a struggle against their natural religious opponents, whom they had always called "Moors" or "Moros," so that the Malay Mohammedans received from them the same name "Moros."

The Moro community is made up of four classes: the *dato* class, or nobles; the privileged class, or free citizens; the subjects of the *dato;* and the slaves. Moro law recognizes these classes and differentiates between crimes committed against one class or the other. Slavery does, no doubt, still exist, but it is of a very mild character and is in the majority of cases more like peonage than slavery. This apparent gross inequality of rights among the people has considerably diminished since American occupation and is gradually dying away.

Moro history and Moro nationality according to Moro tradition owe their beginning in the Philippine Islands to Abu Bakr, a Mohammedan Arabian born in Mecca. He came to Sulu about A. D. 1450 as a trader and settled at Bwansa, the ancient capital of the island. He soon found favor with Raja Baginda, the local chief, became his judge and high priest, and married his only daughter. At the death of Baginda his talented son-in-law, Abu Bakr, assumed the reins of government under the title of the Sultan of Sulu, and proceeded to form a new kingdom. He taught the former priests Arabic and the Koran, built mosques, and baptized the chiefs and the masses as Mohammedans. He organized the state, assigned the territories and duties of chiefs, and levied taxes and tribute from all of them. He reformed the laws of the people, prepared and published the first code, and established a system of courts. He united the various districts and islands into one sultanate and joined all the diverse elements of the Sulu Archipelago into one nation.

The dynasty founded by Abu Bakr ruled with a firm hand and attained considerable power and fame. The new organization, establishing law and order, consolidated the forces of the state, and increased its influence on the outside world. Islam added a new element of strength and another stimulus to campaign and conquest. The Sulus never exceeded 60,000 in number, yet we learn that, prior to the arrival of Magellan, their power was felt all over Luzon and the Visayan Islands, the Celebes Sea, Palawan, North Borneo, and the China Sea, and their trade extended from China and Japan, at one extreme, to Malacca, Sumatra, and Java at the other. What Abu Bakr did for Sulu was probably greater than what Raja Brooke did for Sarawak, though we have never stopped to think of Abu Bakr in this light.

The Moro of the *dato* or privileged classes, reared in his infancy by *panditas* who were wise in Hindu lore, was brought up to maturity under the care of Mohammedan priests. He had been for more than a century prior to the arrival of Legaspi at Cebu, a faithful and devoted worshiper of "Allahu Ta'ala," the Almighty God, according to the teachings of the prophet Mohammed and the holy Koran. He had laws, an organized government, an alphabet, and a system of education. By trade he was planter and fisher, and both land and sea yielded him plenty. He turned the timber of his rich forests into boats and utilized the currents of the sea and the movements of the wind. Navigation came natural to him, and he sailed to distant lands and traded his pearls for silks and spices. He had a fair range of experience and his knowledge of the world was by no means restricted to one island or to one limited group of islands. True, the Moros had no standing army or navy, but they had innumerable boats, forts, and firearms and every able-bodied man was a soldier and a sailor, always armed and always ready for a call to arms. His immediate neighbors were pagans, who paid him homage and tribute. He was the master of the land and the lord of the southern seas. He was chivalrous in his manners, and received his friends with liberal hospitality; but he wasted no sympathy or kindness on his enemy. The enemy of the state was also an enemy to "Allahu Ta'ala," and no life was deemed too dear to sacrifice for the cause of home and God.

No effort was made by Spain to educate the Sulus and no adequate measure was proposed by her Sulu governors which was applicable to the needs of the Sulus and acceptable to their ideas. The Sulus felt that there was a strong inclination on the part of the Spanish government or some of its recognized agents to destroy their national unity, and consequently, they never had complete confidence in Spanish officers and representatives and repulsed every influence that tended to establish close relations between them and the Christians of the Spanish garrison.

No tax or tribute was collected from the Moros, and their territory was exempted from the operation of the laws of the Philippine Islands. Sulu imports could come in Sulu craft free of duty and unhampered by any regulation. Duties could be collected by the Sultan of Sulu at all ports unoccupied by Spain; and if hostilities could have been brought to an end, the Sulus, in their pursuit of the peaceful vocations of life, might have felt no appreciable difficulty or inconvenience from Spanish occupation of Sulu except the loss of the revenues of the ports of Jolo and Siasi and some control over the trade of the Chinese.

Piracy was completely suppressed in 1878, but slavery remained an established institution of the land and its continued practice among the

1. Winding Spun Cotton Thread. Batangas Province. Luzon
Note the use of the toes to maintain even tension on the bobbin.

2. Reeling Abacá Fiber, Pototan, Iloilo

1, A Negrito Shelter, Zambales Province, Luzon

2. Habitation of a Bontoc-Igorot Family, Mountain Province,
Luzon

1. BUTBUT, AN IGOROT VILLAGE, MOUNTAIN PROVINCE, LUZON

2. IGOROT WOMAN WITH PACK BASKET, MOUNTAIN PROVINCE, LUZON

The growing of tubers yielding starchy foods such as taro, *gabi,* which is piled high in the basket, is common to the upland Indonesian peoples of Luzon.

PLATE 12

1. TINGUIAN HUNTERS, ABRA, NORTHERN LUZON

The pagan Tinguian continues to use with a plain hardwood bow an ancient form of Indonesian composite arrow.

2. A BONTOC-IGOROT, MOUNTAIN PROVINCE, NORTHERN LUZON

Fastened in his hair and suspended over his right ear he carries a brass pipe. In his hands he holds weapons of his own manu-

Moros was neither vigorously denounced nor effectively restricted. The pearl industry remained in the hands of the Sulus and pearl fishers and shell dealers paid a variable tax to the sultan and the local chiefs.

Brass cannon, the pride of the Moro soldier, were effective enough against other Filipino tribes not possessing firearms. Respect for the fighting qualities of the Moro was bestowed by the Spanish also on the small cannon or *lantaca* of native Moro manufacture. The Spanish, however, attributed them to Bornean or Chinese origin. These small culverins have a bore of from 1 to 2 inches. They were mounted on a single swivel bar and placed on the stockades, forts, and war praus (*prahus*) of the Moro. As other Mohammedanized Malays of western Malaysia employed similar cannon and as the entire war complex of the Moro was derived from the Asiatic mainland through the agency of the Saracen missionary, it is probable that both the knowledge of making gunpowder and brass cannon came not from China, as was believed by the early Spanish, but from Arabia by way of the island chain of western Malaysia.

At the arrival of the Spanish, natives of Borneo exchanged in trade with the Filipinos many articles which they themselves had obtained from China and India. Such merchandise included copper and tin, porcelain, dishes, gongs, bells, and cooking vessels of metal from China; cloth and blankets from India; and iron lances, blades, and knives, which were derived either from India or had been fashioned by the natives of Borneo. Slaves, beeswax, gold, shells, and cloth were received from the Filipino in exchange. Junks from Siam trading with the Visayan Islands were encountered by the Spanish. Malays sent their war praus to trade with islands as remote as northern Luzon. Legaspi while at Bohol Island engaged in battle with one of these trading vessels belonging to the southern or Mohammedan Moro. "Everywhere in the vicinity of Manila ("Maynila"), on Lubang, in Pampanga, at Cainta and Laguna de Bay, the Spaniards encountered forts mounting small cannon, or 'lantakas'." (Relacion de la Conquista de la Isla de Luzon, 1572, *in* Retana, Archivo del Bibliofilo Filipino, vol. 1.)

Not only firearms but the art of casting brass weapons had been acquired by the Moro along with the art of making gunpowder. Morga's account of the conquest of Manila in 1570 by Martin de Goiti, and of the small islands of Lubang near Mindoro by Salcedo (Sucesos de las Filipinas), relates how the Moro had strong forts with high walls on which were mounted brass cannon. Moats surrounded these forts. It is interesting to note that the Mohammedan Moro defender of Manila was known as a *raja* (Hindu), and that after the battle the body of a Portuguese artillerist who had aided in the defense was found among the dead. The Moro *rajas* continued the struggle against the Spaniard and gathered a fleet of 40 war praus which assembled in the nipa-palm-inclosed estuaries of the Pampanga and other rivers flowing into Manila Bay. The armor and offensive weapons of the Spanish, consisting of mailed steel, heavy swords, long lances, and firearms, prevailed over the inferior shields, armor, guns, spears, and arrows of the Moro. An interesting event in the battle was the cooperation of the natives of the village of Macabebe, in what is now Pampanga Province, with the Moro *rajas.* The Macabebe have ever since proved a recruiting ground for the armies of Spain and later of America. A group of Macabebe accompanied General Funston on his famous expedition which resulted in the capture of Gen. Emilio Aguinaldo. The Macabebe, like the Sikhs of India, contributed more than their quota of soldiers for the army of occupation.

For centuries the Moro pirate has been the scourge of the navigator in the waters of the East Indies. Dyak and Moro alike relied more on individual courage and fighting ability than on mere strength of numbers, equaling in their courage and in the extent of their exploits the feats of the English privateers, Drake and Cavendish. Moro piracy continued, disturbed from time to time by the Spanish, but not to be broken up until the arrival of the first steamships in Philippine waters in 1848 made possible the pursuit of the Malay war praus. It had been possible for the praus manned by oarsmen before this time to drop their masts on the approach of a vessel with superior armament and to turn toward the "eye of the wind," where it was impossible for a sailing vessel to follow. The Spanish governor, Claveria, with a force of Spanish and Filipino volunteers, entered the pirate country and landed on the island of Balangingi of the Samal Moro, between Jolo and Basilan islands. The Samal are known throughout Malaysia as *bajau* or *orang laut* (men of the sea). Four fortifications were found in the mangrove-covered island. An interesting fact is the large number of brass cannon (124) captured at the time. The activities of James Brooke in his 140-ton armed yacht destroyed the force of the Malay pirates along the north and west coasts of Borneo in 1841.

As late as 1904 the Seranaya expedition, commanded by Maj. Gen. Leonard Wood, encountered the Moro of the Rio Grande Valley, Mindanao, under the leadership of Datto Ali at Seranaya, a Moro fortress and stronghold, to the number of 6,000. This fort (*cota, cotta, kota*), was the greatest military work ever constructed by natives of the Philippine Islands. Dr. Edgar A. Mearns is authority for the statement that on the day of its capture, March 11, 1904, he was able to count 56 mounted cannon and 59 embrasures that were empty or, rather, contained gun carriages from which the guns had been hastily dismounted. Nearly all the guns were subsequently found buried in the moats surrounding the fort or in the ground. The guns were exploded or fired by using the Moros' black powder.

Many of the lantakes or bronze cannon formerly employed by the Moro were cast at Brunei, north Borneo, where the brass and bronze industry is rather well developed, although the fact is well known that the Moros are quite capable of manufacturing such weapons themselves.

THE NEGRITO

The Negrito is usually referred to as the earliest immigrant to the Philippines. The reasons cited in making this assertion are geographical, cultural, and racial. The Philippine Negrito is a member of a race that has everywhere been associated with the forested uplands of the continent or island group in which it dwells. The first census of the Philippine Islands classified these backward people as either Igorot or as Bukidnon (hill people). Each of these terms is now applied to a separate and distinct tribe: the first, Igorot, to an Indonesian tribe occupying a limited area in northern Luzon, and the second, the Bukidnon, to a pagan Indonesian tribe living in the island of Mindanao. The Negrito lives in widely scattered regions in Luzon, Mindanao, Palawan, and other islands. The Tagalog, dwelling in the central plains of Luzon, speak of the Luzon Negrito as the Aeta, Eta, or Atta. The Palawan Island Negrito hybrid is called Batak. This term should not be confused with the Battak of north Sumatra. Gathered here and there in limited numbers in the mountainous areas of southern and eastern Luzon, in Samar, Bohol, Negros, Palawan, Panay, and eastern Mindanao there exist remnants of the same Negrito stock.

If one includes the Negrito-Filipino hybrid element which is for the most part usually reckoned a part of the non-Negrito stock often referred to as the *remontados* (outlaws), together with all tribes possessing Negrito blood, the total number living in the Philippines scarcely exceeds 30,000. Characteristic of the Negrito is his diminutive size, his frizzy hair, his black skin color, and his meager culture. He may be considered as a true pygmy with an average height of less than 145 centimeters (4 feet 9 inches). Similar Negrito types are present in some of the other sections of Indonesia, notably in the interior of the Malay Peninsula. Pygmy Negritos also inhabit the southern portion of the mountainous interior of the island of New Guinea. The racial affiliations of the Negrito lie with the black peoples of Melanesia and Africa, although he is decidedly broad-headed, which the African Negro is not.

One explanation of the separate physical stocks existing in the Philippines lies in the recognition of the fact that their migrations must have occurred at widely removed dates. The Negritos probably came first, the Indonesians later from widely separated dispersal points, and presumably in superior numbers, the protohistoric Malay sporadically, at a still later date. In some of the other large islands of Indonesia a similar sequence of events is indicated. It is also striking that the same juxtaposition of habitat of these same three stocks occurs in Sumatra and also in Borneo, where the aboriginal Negrito has long been a dweller of forested, mountainous terrain in scattered and inaccessible regions, surrounded by the brown-skinned pagan Indonesians, who also dwell in the mountainous interior, while the more roving, seafaring Islamized Malay occupies the coast and the interior river valleys. No confirmation is available of the theory generally advanced that the Negrito has been pushed out of coastal lowlands. It is more likely that his food-gathering habits can best be satisfied in the mountainous regions of the several islands where he has long lived in an almost identical geographical environment.

Local modifications of the Negrito racial type may be observed at many places in the Philippines, where admixture of Indonesian Filipino blood may be traced through the occupation of contiguous areas by representative Filipino groups through a long period of time. There the hybridization of the Negrito occurs to a greater or less extent on the borders of their respective territories. The striking thing is the clear-cut distinction in racial type which does exist despite many centuries of miscegenation, and despite the almost complete loss of all trace of the original Negrito language and culture trait complex.

More Negritos are found in the Philippine Islands than elsewhere in Indonesia; also more Negritos are found in Luzon than in all the other islands of the Archipelago together. The Luzon group, largest in numbers and probably purest in type, occupies the Zambales mountain range embracing the larger part of the mountainous region of the provinces of Bataan, Zambales, Pampanga, and Tarlac. This Bataan group, numbering about 6,000 souls, is somewhat further advanced in civilization than are the Negritos of other parts of the Philippines. They live for the most part in permanent, self-supporting communities, dividing their time in the chase, in the cultivation of maize, tobacco, and vegetables, and gathering of forest products for trade with coast people. They are known locally as Aeta. Their dialect is a corrupt form of Zambal, the language of the Indonesian Filipino inhabitants of Zambales, though in regions in close proximity to other dialects, it, in turn, has become mixed with Tagalog, Pampanga, or Pangasinan. The Negritos living on Mount Mariveles in Bataan Peninsula are among the most primitive of all human beings and are a mild and peaceful people. They fish and hunt, and live on wild bananas, coconuts, papaya, snakes and crocodiles. During the recent furious struggle at Bataan, these aborigines, terrified by the savagery of civilized man, retreated to the comparative security of the great rocky crater of Mariveles.

Besides the Zambales mountain groups, Negritos are found in 11 or 12 other provinces of Luzon. In Sorsogon and Albay at the southern end of Luzon there are a few scattered families of mixed types, living near or among the Bikol population. In the vicinity of Mount Isarog, in the Camarines, there is a much larger number running wild in the mountains, but they also are of mixed blood. Negritos are found pretty well scattered over Tayabas; in the northern part they approach more clearly to a pure type. In these provinces they are known locally under a variety of names, as Agta, Aeta, Baluga, and Dumagat. All along the eastern coast of Luzon, in Isabela and Cagayan Provinces, there are large numbers of Negritos. This eastern coast region of northern Luzon is yet to be explored, but information so far received shows that the Negritos have intermingled with the primitive mountain Indonesian, and that they live a wild, wandering life, subsisting largely on game, edible roots, and wild fruits. This hostile coast has been settled but little by the more civilized Filipinos, but where the latter have established themselves the Negritos near them have borrowed something of their customs and are more disposed to a permanent residence, cultivating small crops of their own and working for the Filipinos. In the western half of northern Luzon there are only one or two small groups of Negritos, as in Abra and Ilokos Norte.

In the southern islands, Panay stands next to Luzon in the number of its Negrito inhabitants. They are known as Ati, and are found all over the interior mountainous portion of the island.

In Negros, the island which presumably takes its name from the large number of Negritos living there in early times, the Negrito population is now very small, and is confined to the extreme southern and northern regions. These Negritos have preserved their wild life, are therefore free from mixture with the Visayan Filipinos, and are rapidly disappearing.

The question as to the origin of the Negrito is a debatable one. Unfortunately, conclusive archeological evidence as to the geographical source of this pygmy black race does not exist. We find remnants of the Negrito occupying secluded interior areas in Luzon, Mindanao, and other Philippine Islands as well as in neighboring islands. In appearance, the Negrito's resemblance to certain pygmy African tribes is striking. Presumably also, his early migrations were without the aid of advanced types of boats. Nowhere is the Negrito a good boatman or builder of boats, his major achievement being, perhaps, crudely hollowed-out logs not at all comparable in design and seaworthiness to the smaller of the Filipino outrigger boats. It is suggested that the distribution of the Negrito may have occurred at a very remote time when the Malay Peninsula was, at any rate, still connected with Sumatra and the other Sunda Islands. If this assumption is granted, a further assumption must be made that the larger Philippine Islands were connected and the Negritos' migrations were practically all by land.

The Chinese writer, Chao Ju-Kua, in the thirteenth century, was the first to give a written description of the Negrito. The statement is usually made by ethnologists that the Negrito was formerly more numerous and that he occupied most of the archipelago. There is no proof for this, although on the island of Luzon, for example, he continues to occupy widely separated habitat ranges in the neighboring provinces of Bataan and Zambales, the more remote Tayabas, Camarines, and much of the distant northeastern mountainous fringe of the island in the provinces of Cagayan, Isabela, and Nueva Vizcaya. Furthermore, the nomadic habits of the Negrito, which tend to make him a mountaineer and a collector of food rather than a producer of agricultural crops, all lead to the contrary assumption that the Negrito population never was great and that it never extended beyond what to him is a natural habitat, namely, the mountainous forested areas of the islands.

The Negrito rarely plants a food crop and still more rarely remains in one location long enough to harvest what he has planted. He lives in small bands of closely related family groups. He has no domesticated animals other than the dog and a few mountain chickens used as decoys in trapping wild fowl. The Negrito house is a crude structure made by driving into the ground small poles with forked tops. Sticks are laid across these forks which serve as a support for a brush or thatched roof. The sides of the house are not enclosed. Basketry mats are used as beds. A smudge fire is maintained to keep away insect pests and to supply warmth. The Negrito is prone to sleep in the ashes of these fires and consequently bears scars from burns contracted by too close contact with live coals and hot ashes.

The Negrito kindles a fire by means of the two-piece bamboo fire saw, an art in which he is adept. He cooks his food slightly in a vessel consisting of a cut section of bamboo stem. Other sections of the bamboo stem also serve as containers for drinking water and for food such as grubs or wild honey that he has collected in the forest.

The clothing of the Negrito is scanty. What little is worn is fashioned from the beaten inner bark of a tree. This bark cloth is worn by the women sarong-fashion around the waist and by the men as a breech clout. The cortex or outer surface of combs made of bamboo, and of containers used for various household purposes, is decorated with incised angular patterns. These decorative patterns form one of the few pleasing phases of Negrito material culture. Bodily ornamentation, accomplished by raising scar tissue in patterns resembling the totemic cicatrization marks of West African Negro tribes, is obtained by the use of bamboo knives. The Negrito, like many pagan Filipino groups, sharpens his teeth to points. This practice, however, is not general and is clearly a borrowed trait. Leglets of pig bristles are woven and worn by the men. This type of bodily ornamentation may be one of the few surviving true Negrito culture traits.

The bow and arrow is his chief hunting weapon, although game may also be trapped or snared. The use of the blowgun, a weapon borrowed from the pagan Filipino, is limited to the Negritos of the island of Palawan. Even the poisoned darts are identical in structure with those fashioned by the Indonesian Toala on the island of Celebes for use in their blowguns. The Negrito blowgun, however, is not of the two-piece hollowed-wood type which is grooved and fitted together carefully, wrapped, and provided with separate mouthpiece such as that produced by the Jacuns of the Malay Peninsula. The Negrito blowgun of the island of Palawan is of much simpler construction and is essentially hollowed cane, which is, however, decorated with spiral markings effected by burning, and is provided with a fitted mouthpiece.

Negritos of Bataan still frequent, and have been referred to as formerly living on, the island of Corregidor, within sight of the great city of Manila. Zuñiga in 1803 wrote that the Negritos living in the vicinity of Angat, Bulacan Province, scarcely more than 50 miles from Manila were head hunters. Dean Worcester also refers to the Negritos of the northeastern coast of Luzon as head hunters carrying the head ax on their journeyings.

The original language, as well as the entire culture complex of the Negrito, remain and probably will continue to remain unknown. In every instance where the Negrito language and culture have been expertly examined, it has been clearly established that both were borrowed from neighboring Filipino groups. The language spoken by most of the Negritos of northern Luzon is Ibanag—the language of the Cagayanes of the Cagayan Valley. The explanation for this, of course, may be found in the fact that the northern Luzon Negrito mingles somewhat with the Ilocanos and Cagayanes of northern Luzon and has casually adopted their language, which is, presumably, useful in their meager trade relations.

Borrowed culture traits, however, place the Negrito closer to the Kalinga and Isinai who, like the Negritos, are a mountain people of mixed composition but nevertheless not related racially to the Negrito. The Negritos are accustomed to the wearing of earrings resembling those of the Kalinga. To illustrate further the Negritos' propensity of borrowing culture traits, it may be noted that the Negritos, in contact with the Isinai, practice, like the latter, male circumcision or incision, whereas those living near the Kalinga, among whom circumcision is rare, do not practice it. Also, a ceremonial dance of the Negritos who live near the Isinai is an Isinai dance.

Comparisons of temperament are perhaps not susceptible to statistical or other scientific checks so that when it is stated that the "Negrito is volatile, vivacious and impulsive while the Malay is reserved and restrained," the thought conveyed by such a statement may be merely subjective, since emotional restraint is in many cases itself a cultural trait rather than a physical one.

Peculiarities in borrowing of culture traits are further noted by the fact that the Negrito remains monogamous while his Isinai neighbor has as many wives as he can afford. With the Negrito, divorce is rare, while among the Isinai there are many grounds for divorce. The Indonesian's fondness for a ceremonial wedding is shared by the Isinai—not so, however, by the Negrito, who has no marriage ceremony at all. The go-between, an Indonesian institution, is not resorted to by the Negrito before entering the marriage relation. Then, in the rearing of children, the usual Filipino practice of carrying the child on the hip has not been adopted by the Negrito mother of the mountain province, who carries her child on the arm or swaddled to her back. The lack of taboos concerning their own names and the names of their wives' relatives is in striking contrast with such taboos existing among the Isinai.

The Indonesian Filipino of the mountain province of northern Luzon has an abundance of religious observances and taboos more definitely characterized as magic. The interpretation of dreams, of omens pertaining to such common occurrences as the entrance of a bird into the house, the blowing of a leaf along the floor, or meeting a snake in the pathway, the divination of animal gall bladders, the wearing of amulets, observance of lucky and unlucky days are shared for the most part by the Indonesian Isinai. The Negrito, his neighbor, however, has no lucky or unlucky days. He observes no omens. The wearing by the Negrito of a pendant similar to the amulet worn by the Indonesian Filipino, is not an amulet to the Negrito but an object of personal adornment—it has no magical powers. Death, which is attributed by the Kankanai, another Indonesian mountain group, to supernatural causes is, to the Negrito, entirely natural. There is, in short, little in the religious culture of the Negrito resembling the animistic beliefs and practices of the Isinai, Kankanai, Kalinga, and Ifugao of the Luzon mountains. There is no trace in the Negrito's religion of ritualism. There is, of course, no shaman. The Negrito, if he mentions it at all, refers to ghosts in the singular as "a ghost"—something definite and natural that he has in mind.

The prevailing Indonesian concept of sacrifice, evidenced by such practices as the pouring of a little rice wine on the ground before drinking, or the more elaborate blood sacrifice of dogs, pigs, and chickens, is shared to a limited extent by the Negrito of the mountain province. His observance, however, of sacrificial practices is sketchy as compared with the more elaborate Indonesian observance of sacrifices by such people as the Bontoc, the Isinai, and even the Christian Ilocano. The survival of the use by the Negrito of a song, the words of which are no longer understood by the Negrito, may point to the existence of a former Negrito language which otherwise has completely disappeared. It is clear that, as in his cultural and linguistic borrowings, the Negrito has also sketchily borrowed some of the much more elaborate magico-religious observances of the animistic Indonesian mountain tribes. The fact that the Negrito has borrowed so ineffectually from the wealth of animistic and superstitious practices of the Indonesian establishes, in the absence of any magico-religious observances of his own, that the Negrito originally, as uninfluenced by neighboring cultures, was a realist depending almost entirely on a cause and effect interpretation of natural phenomena.

THE ROLE OF BAMBOO AND RATTAN

In contrast to the primitive living conditions of the Negritos, the Indonesian culture trait complex reaches even in its lower strata a comparatively high level. In order to understand the culture possessions of the Filipino peoples it is necessary to consider how tremendously important in their daily lives are two plants, bamboo and rattan. The Filipino in the provinces lives in an age of bamboo. His house rests on bamboo piles; all supports, beams, and reinforcements are made of bamboo. The tubular structure of bamboo easily makes possible a type of construction without the use of nails or other binding material. The floor and walls of the house are composed of thin strips of bamboo or of planks shaped from cleaved bamboo tubes. Even the framework of the roof is made completely of bamboo. A layer of halved bamboo stems with the hollow side facing upward is then laid on the framework, and interlocking with these from above there is placed a similar layer with the hollow side facing downward, the completed structure resembling a Spanish roof of tiles. Fences and defensive enclosures are built of cut bamboo stems driven vertically into the ground. When well woven together with horizontal laths of bamboo, the fence serves as an almost impenetrable barrier against marauding pigs. A section of a bamboo stem with lower nodal joint division retained is universally used as a portable water vessel or as a container for storage of drinking water. A section of cut bamboo stem is even employed as a cooking vessel by both the Negrito and Filipino. Dry bamboo supplies excellent fuel. Young bamboo shoots when cooked are excellent for eating and are appreciated by Filipinos and Americans. Furthermore, bamboo tubes of varying thickness supply large and small containers and boxes for all sorts of uses, as for betel and tobacco, arrow quivers, and knife sheaths. The sharpened bamboo is itself a lance or a spear for hunting and fishing. Path splinters of bamboo of varying length are used for defense, while the bamboo sharpened along its lateral edge serves as a knife and also as a fire saw for fire making, two pieces being rubbed rapidly across each other at right angles. The hollow bamboo reed led to the invention of the blowgun, which was later fashioned out of wood. The bamboo reed furnishes in simplest form a music instrument—the Malay flute. Sounding holes or vents are spaced to form the desired tones pleasing to the Filipino ear. The Malay tonal sequence is quite different from our diatonic musical scale. Bamboos bound together with undisturbed nodal joints forming air pockets form a natural float of considerable carrying capacity. The superior divisibility and flexibility of bamboo is utilized in native and loomless weaving of mats. The serviceability of the Filipino fish weir depends on the flexibility of bamboo and on the ease with which it can be split into sections. Interwoven bamboo lattices are fashioned in every desirable length and breadth for the walls of the house, for closing open gables, for bridges, and other substantial uses. The seaworthiness of the Filipino dugout sailing banca is unthinkable without its bamboo single or double outrigger. The tubelike nature of bamboo led of itself to its use by the Bontoc and the Ifugao for water conduits in rice-terrace irrigation and for water wheels in lowland rice culture, also in the primitive double bellows used by the Filipino ironworker.

Of equal utility in Filipino material culture is the reed rattan palm, *Calamus mollis.* Because of its flexibility and tensile strength it is a building material without comparison. The native of the interior uses neither iron ferrules nor nails in construction work, and there are probably few articles of use on which rattan bindings do not appear.

The prominent properties of bamboo and also of rattan can only be utilized when in possession of tools of a material with which one can work them, namely, iron or steel. Stone implements cannot be used on the brittle cortex of bamboo or the tough fiber of rattan. Among the early Polynesians and other Oceanic peoples living essentially still in the stone age, bamboo plays only a small role. We must therefore reckon the use of bamboo and rattan as one of the characteristic achievements of the iron age in primitive Filipino culture.

HABITATIONS

All types of Filipino houses are derived from the rectangular pile dwelling with gable roof. Other forms of construction are based on borrowed architectural forms derived from Asiatic or European sources.

Among Indonesians outside the Philippine Islands—for example, in Engano and certain other isolated localities—round huts are built. This type of habitation is unknown in the Philippines. A large percent of the Javanese live in houses that are built directly on the ground, a custom that certainly was taken over from the Hindus. Dwellings that are erected on piles above the ground vary enormously in size. In the Philippines, houses ordinarily serve one family, sometimes several families, sometimes an entire village. The size of the structure varies accordingly. From small huts of only a few feet in each dimension, the size extends up to 100 feet in length in communal structures, and in Borneo even exceeds 300 feet in length. In the case of these great communal houses a section is added as needed. Communal village houses are characteristic of primitive Indonesian culture strata as among the Bontoc and Ifugao. The more recent coast population does not build such structures. The raw material used in the construction of the Bontoc and Ifugao house is wood derived from the Benguet pine, *Pinus insularis,* or bamboo. Hewn planks or boards here are substituted for the bamboo of the lowlands.

Characteristic also is the differentiation of the houses according to their use. In addition to the family houses, there are special bachelor houses, mostly similar in construction but with more open walls that often consist of strong planks. Here the bachelors and visitors that come to the village sleep and here the men spend the greater part of the day. Here also is the forum for discussions and the dispensing of justice. In war, these bachelor houses become natural fortresses. Similar houses erected for unmarried women are more unusual, and in the Philippines the practice is limited to Igorot peoples of the mountain province in northern Luzon. In addition to these, there are houses of the dead, as among the Manobo in eastern Mindanao, that stand in the village or a short distance apart. Sometimes small, sometimes larger, they are built according to the prevailing type of dwelling occupied by the living. The ever-present storage houses for foods, as rice and sweet potatoes (*camotes*), also roughly resemble tribal dwellings.

The Bontoc-Igorot of the mountain province live in towns compactly built and large, the people depending upon numbers in resisting the attacks of their enemies. All approaches to the town were formerly guarded by sentries. Each town was divided into a number of *atos*, or wards, every inhabitant belonging to one or another *ato*. At some convenient point in each *ato* were erected the following structures: (a) an open stone court at some height above the adjacent ground, where out-of-door councils of the old men were held; (b) a long, low building, usually divided into two rooms, one of which is used as a council chamber in wet weather, the other for secret consultations and as a burial place of the heads of victims killed in war after suitable festivities have been celebrated; (c) a long, low building in which unmarried girls are obliged to sleep at night; (d) a similar building in which sleep boys and unmarried men, or men who have lost their wives.

Set in or near the stone court are stakes with their upper ends sharpened. Upon these sharpened ends the heads of victims killed in war were impaled, while a feast, varying in length with the importance of the victim and the wealth of his slayer, was celebrated. Thereafter the head was taken down and buried in the secret chamber of the *ato* for 3 years, at the end of which time it was dug up and another feast was celebrated. The dead limbs or posts are often ornamented with the skulls of hogs or water buffaloes (carabao) which have been eaten at *canaos*, or religious feasts. A series of pig pens is usually connected with the *ato*, where hogs are kept ready for sacrifice.

Most of the houses at Bontoc are built on a uniform plan, which the natives say they owe to their god, who descended from a neighboring mountain in order to show them how to construct their dwellings. The side walls do not reach up to the roof, which spreads over them in such a way as to keep out rain and still allow the smoke to be carried away by the free circulation of air. Habitations are rectangular. The entrance is at one end, and on the left as one enters are two cells, one in which food is prepared, and the other in which it is cooked. The family perches on a long bench on the right side of the entrance. The sleeping box made of roughly hewn pine boards extends across the opposite end of the dwelling. The cubicle is 6 to 10 feet in length, 2 or 3 feet in width, and 2 or $2\frac{1}{2}$ feet in height, floored at one end with pine boards, while at the other end a dirt floor is maintained on which to build a fire. The parents and young children lie here at night, kept warm but half stifled by the choking smoke. Under the eaves of the houses firewood is stored at the beginning of the rainy season. Several finished coffins nicely hollowed out of pine trunks are also in evidence.

The tree house of the pagan Gaddang, living in northeastern Luzon, is an extreme type of thatched pile dwelling formerly common in Luzon and Mindanao when the country was not peaceful and the occupants had to protect themselves at night by drawing the ladder up from the ground. The Bagobos of the Gulf of Davao region in southern Mindanao formerly achieved the same type of protection for their habitations by constructing a light bamboo framework house resting on piles extended 20 feet or more above the ground. The exaggerated pile dwelling constituted an improvement over the much smaller tree pile dwelling such as that of the Gaddang which is built into the high crotch of a single tree. Tree houses, except temporary structures used in emergencies or as watch-towers, are no longer built. Permanent tree dwellings were also formerly constructed by the primitive Lubu of central Sumatra.

The Dyaks, who live mainly in the heavily forested interior of Borneo, also build long communal structures erected on high posts with a wide bamboo-floored porch where the household activities are carried on. These houses are built along river courses. Rice storehouses are also built as in the south.

Balinese dwellings are rectangular in ground plan, but the walls are generally of clay, an unusual type of construction in Indonesia. Sasak houses, in Lombok, stand, not on piles, but on stone mounds. Rectangular pile dwellings and structures without piles occur side by side in western Java, in parts of the smaller Southwestern Islands, in Ceram-laut, and in Halmahera. The Indonesian pile dwelling ranges in size from the small single-family Filipino structures to the enormous Borneo longhouses, which often measure hundreds of feet in length.

Deviations from the usual rectangular ground plan occur in a few places. The pile structures of Engano and of western Flores are round; similar ones are found on the Nicobars. The large family houses on the Mentawi Islands often end as a half cupola. Round huts are described as built by the Semang of the Malay archipelago. In the interior of Borneo there are round communal bachelor halls; aside from this occurrence in pronounced marginal areas there exist round structures again in the extreme east of the Indonesian island world, adjoining Melanesia. This survival of a type of negroid "melanesian" round "beehive" dwelling in brown Indonesia is significant.

WEAPONS

As varied as the clothing worn are the kinds of weapons used. Of the primitive weapons are to be mentioned first of all the bow and arrow. Poison-tipped arrows for the chase and for use in war are to be contrasted with the many-pointed fish arrow, in which often the detachable point is fastened by means of a string to the hollow bamboo shaft. In Indonesia the blowgun is limited in its distribution more to the west, particularly in Sumatra, Malay Peninsula, and Borneo; it likewise survives in the western Philippine island of Palawan. Here it is composed of bamboo, sometimes provided with a lance point, and so becomes a weapon for use at both short and long distances. When the bow is used, the long arrows are provided at their lower end with a nock and feathering. With them a hunter can shoot accurately at a distance of 20 to 25 meters.

The shields vary greatly in size and form, and their raw material often corresponds to their particular use. Shields that are to serve for the stopping of arrows are made preferably of soft wood which holds the arrow, while those that are to withstand sword blows or lance thrusts are constructed of the most durable hardwood. Thus a rattan shield withstands every spear thrust. The Asiatic round shield was the customary form in Jolo and to a limited extent in Mindanao, where Mohammedan influence was strong. Pagan peoples of Luzon preferred small elongated forms, while in Mindanao and Celebes appear broad shields, some of which are so large that they completely cover the bearer.

Widespread is the use of the lance, and especially preferred is the throwing lance. Among the cutting weapons two kinds are distinguished: one, a heavy, slender, curved blade that, like our swords, has the main weight in the grip; the other type, the *kampilan* of the Moro and the common *bolo* which harks back to more primitive forms, is straight and broadens toward the point.

PLATE 13

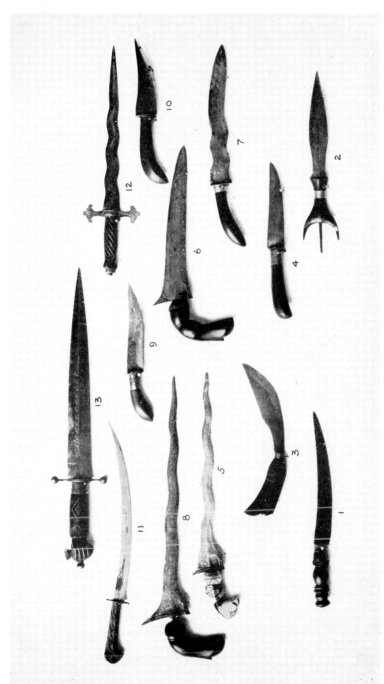

STEEL KNIVES AND DAGGERS

The Filipino ironsmith anciently learned how to forge iron and temper steel. The Moro fabricates the finest blades in artistic designs (Nos. 4-12); weapons of other peoples, No. 1, Visayan, Samar Island; No. 2, Mandayan, southeastern Mindanao; No. 3, Bagobo, southeastern Mindanao; No. 13, Tagalog, central Luzon.

1. BUYO BOX OF CAST BRASS, MORO, WESTERN MINDANAO

Buyo chewing is general. Ornamental brass containers for the areca nut, the chief ingredient, are cast by the Moro and provided with compartments for lime and the betel leaf, other necessary ingredients.

2. ORNAMENTAL FRUIT DISH OF CAST BRASS, MORO, WESTERN MINDANAO

1, A GROUP OF MORO DATOS, SULU ARCHIPELAGO

The Moro, who geographically is nearest the home of the true Malay, approaches the Malay physically and in culture. His elaborate costume, his Mohammedan religion, his Arabic literature are traditionally Malayan.

2. A GROUP OF IBILAO OR ILONGOT

This pagan Filipino people numbering more than 8,000 is rather mixed physically, showing traces of admixture with Negrito, Formosan and other peoples. They present an interesting study in physical types. Nueva Vizcaya Province, northeastern Luzon.

1. BAGOBO WOMAN, DAVAO, SOUTHEASTERN MINDANAO

The Bagobo man and woman are unsurpassed in the ornamentation of their costumes. Applique beadwork on the woman's jacket contrasts with the wax resist or batik decorative design on *tapis* or skirt.

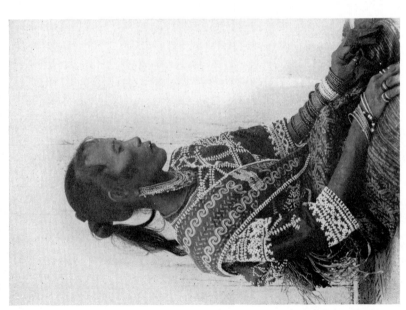

2. SEVERO, A SAMALE HEADMAN OR DATO. SAMAL ISLAND.

The Samal Moro, a deutero-Malayan type, presents a strange contrast in facial features and beard to the general type of Indonesian Filipino. Samal Island belongs to the Jolo or Sulu Archipelago.

These weapons possess a considerable weight forward; their advantage in contrast with the saber is the considerably heavier blow that may be struck. It is easy with such a weapon to cut through a human arm or neck with one blow. Its disadvantage lies in the loss of control of the weapon, even though momentary, that occurs after every blow. Nevertheless, this form of weapon with center of gravity far forward is favored throughout the Islands, and every locality and every Filipino people has its own local variation of it.

Curved war clubs.—Wooden clubs are classified according to their shapes, or according to the nature of the striking end and the method of its employment. They may be straight with plain or ornamented sides; knobbed or bulbous at the striking end; root-ended or curved near the striking end; or they may be expanded into a disklike section at the terminal end. The form into which the club is shaped is probably most often arrived at extemporaneously or independently, so that there is not the same sequence of development from a comparatively simple clubbed weapon to the highly efficient and ornamental types as is the case with metallic cutting weapons or missile weapons. Thus, the war club, *waddy,* of the Australian aborigines is more like a straight unformed stick than are the clubs of any other people. On the other hand, the flat, curved hunting club, the *boomerang,* is a highly specialized form of missile club.

In the islands of the Pacific the wooden club has ranked highest as a war weapon and has retained its position longest. In Melanesia and Polynesia the variety of types, as well as the degree of skill exercised in ornamental carvings and wrappings, have reached their greatest development.

The wooden war clubs of the Philippines were of two kinds, the one probably more ancient than the other. The older type and at the same time the more widely disseminated is the curved or root-ended club. It is usually somewhat bulbous at the striking end and tapers gradually to a grip handle at the base end. The clubs of this type are highly polished and are formed from a hardwood of the molave type. The greatest diameter in section is at the bulbous striking end, from which point a tapered curve of the club is effected so that the terminal end lies nearly at right angles to the body of the club. The club is nearly always octagonal in section, either throughout its entire length or merely at the bulbous striking end.

The spear.—It has been assumed that occupational activities of the different Filipino tribes have to a great extent caused adoption or retention of the bow, the spear, or the blowgun. The bow has been termed the natural weapon of the hunter, while the spear has been adopted by those

tribes that gave up hunting and life in the forest and became agricul-
turalists instead. There is probably some truth and some error in each
of these assertions. The bow is a primitive weapon and was retained by
those tribes that remained primitive forest dwellers and hunters, while
the blowgun is a much more advanced weapon. Both the bow and the
blowgun are designed to increase prehensility of the arm and both employ
the aid of a natural force. The general culture level, however, of the
Filipino and his subjection to higher Asiatic cultures lend probability
to the statement that the blowgun is a primitive Indonesian weapon.
Furthermore, the blowgun was found in general use in the Philippines
along with the spear at the time of the arrival of the Spaniards. The
blowgun is employed by some Negrito tribes, but not by all. For instance,
the Luzon Negritos did not use the weapon. In the same manner that
iron weapons are used by Negrito tribes today whenever possible, they
may formerly have acquired the blowgun. The primitive Negrito-Malay
Batak and Tagbanua of Palawan, the pagan Bagobo, and the Yakan Moro
of today use the blowgun as did the Tagalog and Visayan tribes and other
more civilized Filipino tribes of early Spanish times. The spear is probably older than the blowgun, as the simplicity of its construction in its
most elementary form would seem to indicate. Originally tipped with
bamboo, its shaft was usually constructed of the *palma brava* or of a
bamboo with sharpened end. The notion of fashioning a hollow-tube
blowgun may have originated through the prior use of some hollow-tube
spear. With the advent of iron culture and its more general availability
for such purposes, iron was substituted for the wood or bamboo spear
head. Dr. A. E. Jenks writes that

the head-hunter's battle-ax replaced the spear and the sword in parts of the head-
hunting area of northern Luzon. In this manner, tribal bent was definite. A group
that used the ax employed it consistently and had no swords. The ax cannot be
said to be the earlier form; but it is that which prevailed among the more primitive
tribes possessing least iron and least ability in its manufacture.

The distribution of weapons of offense other than the bow throughout
Indonesia and more particularly within the Philippines follows no one
general principle. Factors contributing to a great variety in design, type
of weapon, materials, and ornamentation seem to vary with each locality
and tribal group. The larger factors of cultural influence, scarcity, or
presence of a plentiful metal supply, and occupational need or tribal
bent combined with a preference for or aversion to hand-to-hand fighting,
are in each group the deciding factors.

The spear was formerly in general use throughout the Philippines.
The wooden spear or one with a bamboo blade gradually lost vogue as

the supply of iron became cheap and plentiful enough to serve as a substitute material. The method of hafting seems to vary with the degree of knowledge of metalcraft possessed by the individual tribal groups. In the northern sections of Luzon, in the Igorot country, the usual method is to insert a metal tang into the wooden shaft. The place of junction is usually strengthened by an iron or braided rattan ferrule. An iron ferrule, spud, or cap is placed over the base end or butt of the shaft for its protection.

Characteristic features of the Negrito bow and arrow.—The bow is the principal weapon of the Negrito in the Philippine Islands and elsewhere in Indonesia, in the Andaman Islands, and in Africa. The bow, as it is usually made by the Negrito, consists of a simple, plain, unwrapped bow stave, rounded in section and often possessing a longitudinally grooved inner surface. It is provided with a bow string of twisted root or bark fiber. The more crudely constructed bows of some of the Malayan Filipino tribes are merely staves of palmwood or of bamboo flattened toward the ends.

The bow, in contrast with primitive clubbing or throwing weapons, is really a primitive gun. It lends increased prehensility to the hand and, when flexed, brings into application a natural force to aid muscular strength. The arrow as a missile weapon lends itself well to the roving and rather furtive life habits of the forest-dwelling Negrito. The Negrito arrow varies with the purpose for which it is to be employed, as for hunting deer and wild pig, for small game, for fishing, and in war. It is either provided with palmwood, bamboo, or iron-tipped points, and is either of simple, compound, or composite harpoon construction.

Antiquity of the bow in Malaysia.—The bow was formerly in general use among the more highly cultured Malayan Filipino peoples as well as among the more primitive Indonesians. Old accounts by various Spanish writers relate how practically all of the Filipino tribes employed the bow. Archers were enlisted or, rather, drafted into service on many of the Spanish expeditions undertaken for purposes of war, conquest, and exploration. Padre Caspar de San Augustin relates that Governor de Sande took with him 1,500 Filipino bowmen from the Provinces of Pangasinan, Cagayan, and the Visayan Islands on his expedition against Borneo. A few years later, in 1593, Governor Dasmariñas had with him Filipino bowmen on his expedition against the Moluccas. Artieda describes large bows employed by the Filipino, more powerful than those of English archers. Some of the Filipino tribes mentioned by early writers as using the bow are the Tagalog of the central Luzon plains, all the pagan tribes of the mountainous region of northern Luzon, as also the civilized Ilocano; the pagan tribes of Mindanao, the Mangyan of Mindoro, the Batak of Palawan, the civilized Bikol of southern Luzon; the Visayan, and Moro—in fact, all tribes, peoples, and nationalities with which contact was established and whose culture consequently became known to the civilized world. The Moro, like many of the other Filipino peoples, continue to use the bow and arrow even at the present time. Formerly, arrows and lances were presented as ceremonial offerings to their deity and were hurled into the waters surrounding Jolo and Zamboanga when the Moro were embarking on an expedition. Some Filipino peoples who have adopted other weapons or who have allowed the use of the bow and arrow to lapse into a subordinate position still use the bow as a toy or in shooting birds or other small game. Dr. A. E. Jenks refers to such secondary use of the bow among the Bontoc-Igorot.

Small boys in Bontok pueblo make for themselves tiny bows 1½ feet or 2 feet long with which they snap light arrows a few feet. But the instrument is of the crudest, merely a toy, and is a thing of the day, being acquired from the culture of the Ilocano who live in the pueblo. The Igorot claim they never employed the bow and arrow, and to-day, at least consider the question as to their ever using it as very foolish, since, they say, pointing to the child's toy, it is nothing. . . . . The Ibalao of the southeastern Nueva Vizcaya, Nueva Ecija, and adjacent Isabella employ the bow constantly.

In an account by Dr. John Frances Careri dating back to 1693-1697, the Zambales nationality is reported as using the bow and arrow, a short spear, and a short hand weapon or knife which was worn at the girdle. The use of poisoned arrows was noted. These arrows were pointed with iron or sharp stones. A peculiarity of the iron arrowheads was in the boring of the head so that it would break off when entering the victim's body. A wooden shield that was twice as long as broad was attached to the arm by horizontal wooden supports at the back of the shield. This shield was employed both for parrying and as a target.

Some of the older types of war arrows of the Moro are very similar to ancient Zambales arrows in that the head, consisting either of stone, metal, bone, or ivory, comes off in the wound made by the arrow. The arrowhead is sunk into or socketed over the foreshaft so that the shaft may become detached while the arrowhead remains in the wound.

The Malaysian self-bow: parts, function, materials.—The type of bow used in the Philippine Islands is the self-bow; it is not reinforced. The flat bows of the southern islands are often wrapped with ornamental transverse windings of rattan splints and the overlay is then waxed with a black gummy cement. As the bow stave is of palmwood in both the wrapped bow and in the unwrapped, and as the stave is usually formed in the same manner—convexly rounded in section toward the outer or front side and flat or concave on the inner side—it appears that the wrapping is purely ornamental and is not a survival of an older type of Asiatic composite bow with its layers of reinforcement. The bow is always held vertically by the Negritos and by the Malayan bowmen. The bow stave is usually longer than the height of the archer. This applies also to the Moro and to those nationalities that have adopted the use of the horse. In their case the introduction of horses did not lead to the shortening of the bow, whereby it could be used to advantage in hunting from horseback as was the case with the North American Indian. This does not imply that the Filipino bow did not gradually assume specialized functions, but specialization in Filipino weapon production reached its greatest extent in the manufacture of metallic hand weapons for cutting and slashing. In this one may see environmental factors, the forest and the tropical climate, operative. The bow, however, remained relatively rather crude and obsolescent except among the primitive Negrito tribes, whose livelihood depends upon the skillful use of this weapon upon which their best efforts and greatest skill are lavished.

Philippine arrow poisons.—The well-known practice of poisoning the tips of the tiny missile darts shot from the *sumpitan* or blowgun is repeated by several Filipino tribes and peoples. In Java and other Indonesian islands the juice of the upas tree is employed for this purpose. The sap of the upas tree is procured by boring a hole in the trunk. Small containers made from a joint of a bamboo stem are filled with the creamy liquid; they are then tightly closed so as to exclude the air. When exposed to the air it rapidly turns black. The arrow or dart point is simply smeared with the juice; if it is fresh, the wound is sure to be fatal; if exposed to air the virulency of the poison seems to be greatly diminished.

Raymond F. Bacon [1] reports some results of experiments conducted on Philippine arrow poisons. He finds that the sap of *Antiaris toxicaria* Leschenault is identical with the sap of the upas tree. This poisonous sap is used on blowgun arrows by the Tagbanua of San Antonio Bay, near the southern end of the island of Palawan. On the island of Mindoro the native use of this material for the poisoning of arrows has been noted near Bulalacao. The Negritos of Bataan Province on the island of Luzon are reported as employing the bark and sap of two trees, the *Diospyros canomoi* and the bicag, in the production of arrow poison. Various other poisons are produced from fermented pineapple leaves and animal poisons, none of them, however, rivaling in strength the antiaris poison extracted

---

[1] Philippine Journ. Sci., vol. 3, No. 1, February 1905.

from the upas, the use of which on the blowgun darts is quite sufficient to bring down and to kill some of the larger animals.

The crossbow.—Built-up bows are made by the Moro who use them as crossbows. The bow stock is composed of two or three pieces of springy, close-fibered wooden strips, wrapped or bound together with wood splints, corded fibers, or hide strips. Such a bow stave is generally connected with a gunstock, which is composed of finely finished hardwood and is provided with the proper triggers made of wood, wire, or bone for gripping and releasing the bow cord.

In Asia the crossbow occurs both in China and in Japan; also in the hill country of Burma, in north Siam, and in Assam. The Aino of northern Japan make a crossbow set as a spring trap in hunting bears. In the Nicobar Islands the crossbow is used as a gun for shooting birds. It is their only type of bow. A toy crossbow, brought by Dr. W. L. Abbott from the island of Simalur off the south coast of Sumatra, has an ingenious arrangement of the bolt which is placed in a groove within a hollow joint of bamboo. The crossbow of the Philippine Islands seems to have been widely distributed in the past and to have been much modified in its form and usage through contact with the Chinese and the Spanish. These modifications consist chiefly in the use of the Chinese repeating crossbow with its movable block magazine; also in the shaping of the crossbow stock and the trigger release made after the fashion of the Spanish rifle.

Blowgun or sumpitan.—The blowgun is primarily a forest weapon. Its use against man or the larger beasts of prey is practically unknown. The reason for this is to be sought in the structure of the weapon and in the nature of its missiles. It is preeminently an effective weapon against small birds or small animals such as monkeys, where stealth and absolute silence are required to make a shot effective. A native walking along a forest path can detect from the traces left on the ground, such as fragments of nuts, etc., the presence of game birds or monkeys high up in the tree tops. A shot from the blowgun may become effective, the game bagged, and the hunter ready for the next opportunity all in perfect silence. This is possible because the poisoned dart causes no outcry such as would be heard if some other missile were employed.

The darts are always light and their range short. A pith or cotton plug causes the dart to fit closely in the tube—a necessity because the missile depends for its expulsion from the tube on the sudden release of compressed air from the mouth of the operator.

The blowgun has enjoyed a wide distribution in the past, though it survives chiefly in Borneo, Malay Peninsula, and in northern South America. The principles involved in its construction and operation seem to imply that it is a weapon of very ancient lineage and represents a wide range of diffusion. Although primarily a forest weapon of Malaysia and tropical America, it formerly appeared on both the east coasts of Asia, including Japan, and in eastern North America as far north as the area occupied by the Iroquois. The American form consists essentially of two grooved halves fitted together with a nicety and wrapped with spiral lashings of flexile basketry material, then coated with wax on the outside. The more common form of blowgun occurring in Indonesia consists of two tubes, one inside the other. The inner tube is formed from an unjointed reed placed within an outer palm or bamboo tube and joined with wax. A basketry wrapping cover and the American type of grooved tube are not unknown.

Use of the blowgun by the Negrito.—As employed by the Negritos, such as the Batak of Palawan, the blowgun is subsidiary to the bow. When hunting for fresh meat, Negritos will send a pack of dogs skirmishing into the forest until a deer is startled from cover. As it dashes wildly by, the little forest pygmies shoot at it with missiles from their bows. The deer continues running pursued by dogs until it falls. Before consuming the meat, however, the priest, *babalian,* or headman offers the entrails to the spirits that have rewarded their efforts.

The blowgun is an effective weapon in the hands of the Negrito in obtaining such game as birds and monkeys. Like the primitive users of the blowgun in South America and Malaysia, the Batak relies on stealth and the effect of his poisoned darts to paralyze temporarily the game that he has silently approached. The poisoned darts are alkaloid and the poison is supposed not to contaminate the flesh of the animal shot. A pygmy Batak will aim his blowgun at a monkey in a tall tree, and with a sudden puff of air from his lips send the dart on its way. The monkey may seemingly remain uninjured until the poison takes effect, when it drops to the ground. Larger game with thicker skins must be killed with an arrow that can penetrate more deeply. The nomad Negrito possesses bows of excellent workmanship, which, together with his quiver of arrows and his other weapons consisting of blowgun and darts, a knife, and a bolo or two, constitute his most valuable and practically his only possessions.

The blowgun, *sumpitan* (Malay), is a remarkable weapon in many respects, and especially because it is one of the few inventions of uncivilized peoples utilizing the force of compressed air; others being the popgun, the fire piston, and the piston bellows. It appears that these inventions are coterminous in range and are products of Malay inventiveness.

5

FOOD AND AGRICULTURE

Philippine economy is founded on agriculture. Rice is the principal cultivated plant. Upland rice is cultivated in dry fields, while other varieties are grown on fields under water. Besides rice, the products of the field—maize especially and sweet potatoes—are important food crops. Of real importance is gardening, which produces sugarcane, bananas, tobacco, vegetables, and utilitarian plants of wide variety.

Rice and vegetables, with little change, form the three daily meals, although fish lends some variety. Among the fruit trees, the palms (coconut, areca nut, etc.) take first rank, but the most prized fruit of all is the durian. It is valued by the aborigines as much as by the forest animals. The number of other fruit trees is truly enormous. The Philippine mango, best known only in the Islands since it is too perishable for export, is the most remarkable for its excellent qualities. Several Spanish governors are said to have exerted great effort to send mangos to their queen but with indifferent success.

Among the domestic animals chickens and the water buffalo, each originally living in a wild state in the jungles and swamps, take first rank; in addition may be mentioned the horse, sheep, pig, goat, dog, cat, not to mention the gecco or house lizard and the house snake. In their passion for gaming, the Malays have developed a breed of game cocks, also special varieties of doves for exploitation in competitive fights. Renowned strains of game cocks were and continue to be classed by the Filipino among the cherished imports from great native trading centers such as Brunei in northwest Borneo.

The assimilation of western ideas has progressed slowly in regard to food habits and predilections. Rice and fish are still supreme, although wheat flour, which has to be imported, is consumed in considerable quantity. During the rainy season, when local fishing is not satisfactory, the demand for canned fish from America increases. Although the Filipinos are not particularly fond of meat, the native use of the meat of the carabao, or water buffalo, goat and kid, pig, and chicken antedates the arrival of the Spanish. Neither the milk of the carabao, which is rich, nor that of the goat is consumed by the adult Filipino. Milk is a medicine or for children. Hunting for game such as waterfowl and wild chickens, and also fishing, are done at night with the aid of torches. Nets are used in catching birds. As in China, roast pig is considered a delicacy not only by natives but by Americans who have been privileged to have it served with a Spanish sauce, the recipe of which is known to every Filipino cook. The *camote,* a mealy variety of the sweet potato, is preferred to the Irish potato, which does not thrive in the tropic lowlands. Minor starchy foods are yams (*ubi*) and taro (*gabe*) and the several palm starches, as that of the sago palm in the Agusan Valley in eastern Mindanao. Special methods of preparing rice, eggs, and other staple foods are pleasing to some foreigners and displeasing to others. Native cooking in any country is a subject on which foreigners are not asked to pass judgment. During especially dry seasons, the agricultural sections of the islands are plagued with swarms of grasshoppers and at yearly intervals with locusts. The native practice is to catch grasshoppers by the use of nets attached to long poles. They are baked and considered delicious. *Balao* or *bagong*, a tiny shrimp, is also caught in nets.

Sprouts from the young bamboo shoots are appetizing and, when boiled, taste like tender asparagus. Many of the most delicious vegetables and fruits known to the Filipino table are too perishable to enter commerce. Included are many varieties of bananas, and above all, the Philippine mango. Refrigerated beef was first imported from Australia for the use of the American Army; later its use spread among the civilians wherever transportation has made regular shipments possible. After all, the common people—the *tao* and his *parientes*—rely on the village market for the purchase of their food supplies.

The Malay institution, the public market, fostered and developed by the Spanish colonial administration, made sanitary and housed in permanent structures under American supervision, has become a center of trade in native foodstuffs and other local produce. As in western countries, the selling of perishable foodstuffs by itinerant venders on street corners has been suppressed, but anyone having something to sell may do so in the village or city market under strict sanitary and police regulations. A government food inspector has become the advance agent of Filipino progress in public sanitation.

Rice is by all odds the principal crop of the western Indonesian peoples including the Filipino, but in the eastern maize and sago zones—the Indonesian islands southeast of the Philippines—it is cultivated either rarely or not at all. The more archaic method of rice cultivation, the caiñgining, which consists in clearing and burning the natural growth in the dry season and planting the grains with digging stick in the ash-covered earth, prevails throughout most of Mindanao, Borneo, and Celebes, and remoter mountain districts of Luzon and Palawan. Irrigated cultivation of rice, either on flat land or on artificially constructed hillside terraces, flourishes in practically all of Luzon, the Visayan Islands, and in a few coastal districts of northwestern Mindanao. All of Java and Sumatra, southwestern Celebes, the Lesser Sunda Islands of Bali, Lombok, Sumba,

Savu, and Roti, and the small Moluccan islands of Ternate and Tidore also have specialized systems of irrigated rice culture analogous to that of the Philippines and to terrace agriculture generally, widely disseminated throughout southeastern Asia from Ceylon to Japan. This more advanced type of agriculture has yet to penetrate the islands off the west coast of Sumatra, the greater part of Borneo and Celebes, most of eastern Indonesia and, in the Philippines, Palawan and the great island of Mindanao. The use of the plow coincides almost precisely with the practice of artificial irrigation, but is dispensed with in the narrow fields of the Bontoc and Ifugao where the steep mountain terraces do not admit of its use.

In densely populated Cebu, however, in parts of Negros and Bohol, and also in certain other districts having soil not adapted to rice and in the tobacco region of Cagayan Valley, maize, not rice, is the chief food crop, while in the diminutive wind-swept Batanes and Babuyanes Islands, north of Luzon, the *camote* (sweet potato), elsewhere a supplementary food, has become the staple.

Fishing contributes vitally to the livelihood of all the coastal dwellers, while hunting holds a definitely subsidiary place in Philippine economic life. Wine, tuba, made from palm sap, when fermented, is a highly intoxicating beverage. Although having an almost universal use in the Islands, the Filipino, like most tropical peoples, has learned to use it sparingly, except when drinking ceremonially as at harvest festivities. The *anitos* and ancestral spirits require due attention and respect even in propitiatory drinking.

LANGUAGE AND THE SYLLABARY

The relationship existing between the numerous living dialects, recognized ethnographic groups or peoples, and their racial origins is one of the most puzzling problems in Philippine anthropology. Following the hypothesis established by Blumentritt and other European scholars, which explains differences in speech, culture, and physical characteristics by assuming a number of migrations to the Philippine Islands from widely separated sources and at various periods, writers have ignored environmental factors. Thus it is noted that the diminutive, black-skinned Negrito whose physical appearance, except for stature, resembles that of the Australian native, invariably speaks the language of his nearest Indonesian neighbor who, in turn, reveals racial characteristics approaching those of the Malay and the southern Chinese.

The number of major migrations to the Philippine Islands is usually established as three: the earliest, in which the Negrito passed into the archipelago over land bridges that have long since disappeared beneath

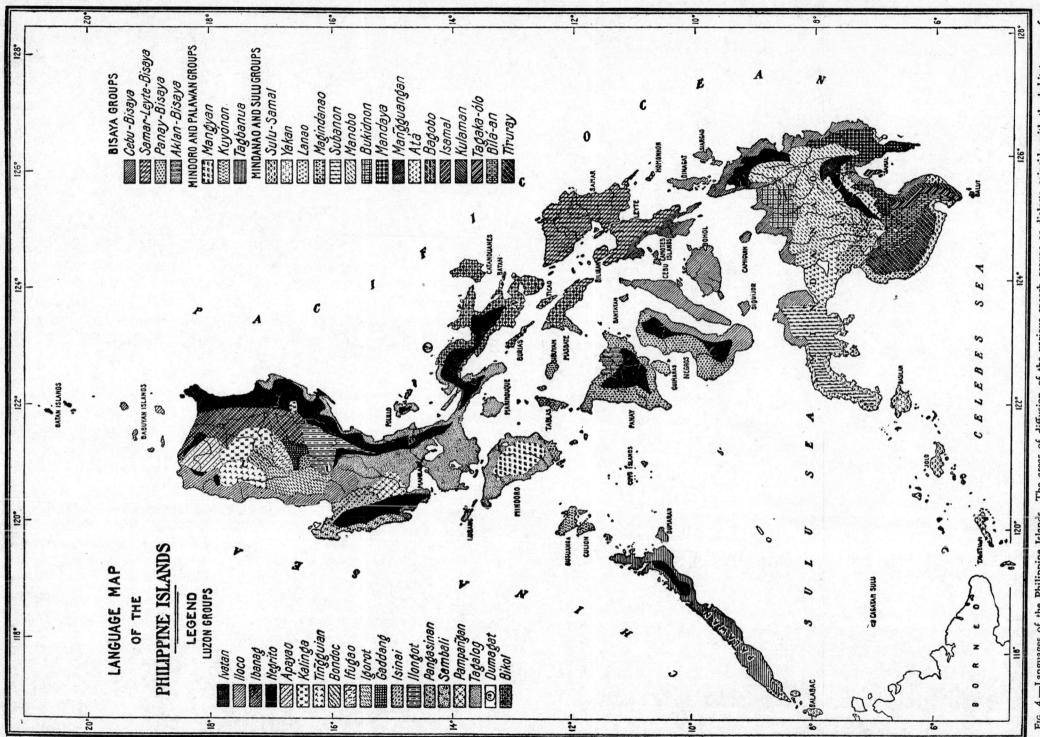

Fig. 4.—Languages of the Philippine Islands. The areas of diffusion of the various speech groups or dialects coincide with the habitat areas of peoples of identical names but do not coincide with the boundaries of political provinces. (From Bull. 2, Philippine Bureau of Science.)

the ocean's surface; the second, that of the proto-Malayan or Indonesian whose presence is characterized by relatively shorter legs, a stocky body, and a general sturdiness not found among representatives of the third migration—those more physically refined peoples, the deutero-Malayans who supposedly came later. Even though occupying widely separated areas, the representatives of the two major posited "Indonesian" and "Malayan" migrations cannot account for a total of 87 speech dialects, for each of which there exist vocabularies and a more or less extensive literature. We must, therefore, either presume a larger number of migrations to the Islands, or account for variations in speech in terms of environmental influences.

Both in speech and culture trait complexes we find sharp distinctions existing among the pagan peoples supposedly ascribable not to racial ancestry or cultural inheritance, but rather to cultural borrowing from more sophisticated or advanced neighboring Christian peoples on the one hand, and geographical isolation or the influence of physical environment on the other. There is no doubt but that the natural ruggedness of the mountain country, the lack of transportation, and difficulty in maintaining trails have isolated ethnic groups and made possible the development of mutually unintelligible dialects. With the development of distinct forms of speech there have been developed fundamental culture trait complexes having to do both with material culture and the organization of society. Thus the Igorot and Ifugao have developed a characteristic type of habitation distinct from that of the Apayao, Kalinga, and Tinguian whose terrain is equally rugged, but whose material culture and social organization are more like that of the neighboring Ilocano.

Notwithstanding the presence of so many distinct dialects, all have been found grammatically related not only to one another, but to the languages spoken in Borneo, Celebes, and elsewhere in Indonesia, as well as to the language still spoken by the native Indonesian tribes of Formosa. Philologists have named this linguistic root Indonesian, and thus by borrowing a geographical term, have extended its boundaries to include all the peoples of Indonesia who speak various forms or dialects of this same root language. Thus, fundamentally, the language of the historic Malay, the Javanese, and the Filipino is one and the same. This underlying unity of speech, with many dialects, to be sure, does not explain the two-fold distinction of Indonesian Filipino peoples into early or proto-Malayan (Indonesian) and later deutero- or historic-Malayans. The more closely related speech groups or dialects are invariably geographical rather than subracial.

Linguists have long known of the distant relationship existing between the speech of all Oceanic peoples including the Filipino, Indonesian, Melanesian, Micronesian, Polynesian, and the distant Indonesian people who long ago occupied the island of Madagascar. The extent of this great Indonesian, or, more basically, Malayo-Polynesian, speech family extends half way round the world. Indonesian or Malayo-Polynesian linguistic relations have been traced to the Mon-Khmer of Indo-China, and the Khasi of Assam on the Asiatic mainland. This discovery may provide a means of establishing the source and the ancient home of the Filipino. The fundamental speech unity within the Philippine archipelago, although obscured by local dialects, is readily understood by the ease with which a Filipino acquires a speaking knowledge of one or more dialects when already familiar with one of them. "Mariano" has been able to broadcast news over KGEI in San Francisco to seven different ethnic groups in the Philippine Islands in as many different dialects.

The speed of culture change of any people is in direct proportion to the complexity of culture traits of the population among whom the acculturation is proceeding. The simpler cultures in the possession of the isolated Negrito groups in Luzon, Panay, and Mindanao have adopted a less number of material culture traits respectively from the Tagalog, Visayan, and Manobo than have been borrowed by the latter peoples respectively from the Christian Spanish and Mohammedan Moro cultures. The substrata of Indian culture trait complex which had penetrated to all the advanced Filipino agricultural peoples of the archipelago made it possible for the Tagalog and the other advanced groups to grasp the fundamentals of Spanish life and of Christian doctrine. These peoples were provided with a language rich in forms and ideas. Long periods of isolation due to primitive transportation and communication and also to separation on the several islands led to the development of fundamental differences in speech and to the formation of many mutually incomprehensible dialects, all of which, however, were grammatically related and shared similar ideologies and word forms. Thus it was possible for the Visayan in a comparatively brief period to master, for example, the Bicol and Tagalog dialects or language spoken on the neighboring island of Luzon. Acculturation once begun has a tendency to accelerate. Changes brought about in the language of the Filipino involve vocabularies and idioms associated with each of the major culture migrations and political systems introduced into the Islands. The mixed vocabulary and idioms of Filipino speech as of the year 1940 are startling. Associated with the rapid increase in the use of English, now, together with Spanish, truly the national language of the Philippine people, are many social changes.

When the Spanish, under Legaspi in 1565, began the Hispanization of the Islands, they found each of the major Filipino peoples literate. A system of syllabary writing was employed closely related to that formerly used in Siam (now Thailand), Cambodia, and Java. In Java, Sumatra, and British Malaya writing is now accomplished primarily in the Malay language written in letters of the Arabic alphabet. The syllabic system of speech recording was derived with intermediate changes direct from India. In lieu of paper, cut strips of pandanus palm leaf were used, and in lieu of a quill, a sharpened piece of bamboo or pointed metal was employed to incise the writing. A variant form of writing "paper" which could be folded like the leaves of a book consisted of palm spathe on which were traced syllabaries with ink. This form of writing, mostly prayer books and genealogies, has been preserved only in rare instances, notably in the University of the Philippines in Manila, and in the United States National Museum in Washington.

The friar Chirino, in his "Relacion de las Islas Filipinas," written in 1602, gives the first Spanish description of the ancient form of writing employed by the Filipino prior to the adoption of the Christian alphabet and the Spanish script, as follows:

So given are these islanders to reading and writing that there is hardly a man, and much less a woman, that does not read and write in letters peculiar to the island of Manila. Very different from those of China and Japan as will be seen from the following alphabet:

The vowels are three; but they serve for five, and are, *a, e,i, o,u.* The consonants are no more than twelve, and they serve to write both consonant and vowel in this form. The letter alone without any point either above or below, sounds with *a.*

With the point placed above, each one sounds with *e* or with *i.* With the point placed below, it sounds with *o* or with *u.* For instance, in order to say *cama,* the two letters indicating the consonants *c* and *m* alone suffice. If to the same consonant letters a point, resembling an apostrophe, is added above each, the word is pronounced *quimi.* If the same cedilla or apostrophe mark is placed below each consonant letter, the word is read *como.* The final consonants are supplied or understood in all cases and the letter is not written. Chirino continues:

. . . . and the reader supplies, with much skill and ease, the consonants that are lacking. They have learned from us (the Spanish) to write running the lines from left and to the right, but formerly they only wrote from above downwards, placing the first line at the left hand, and continuing with the others to the right. Nowadays in writing not only their own but also our letters, they use a quill, very well cut, and paper like ourselves.

The famous Filipino scholar, Dr. Pardo de Tavera, has compiled a considerable number of data regarding early Tagalog, Visayan, Pampangan,

Pangasinan, and Ilocano syllabaries. These are properly not alphabets since the actual letters used are only consonants, the vowels being indicated as mentioned before, by the proper placing of apostrophic cedillas, resembling in this respect the Hebrew script. The source, of course, of the Filipino types of syllabaries is India, whence have been derived not only writing but many Sanskrit words. The old scripts of Sumatra, Java, southwestern Celebes (Macassar and Buginese), Sumbawa, and the Philippines (Tagalog, Visayan, Mangyan, and Tagbanua) are all Hindu Brahmi alphabet. A rather extensive literature of pre-Spanish days thus recorded is known to have existed. The friar Totanes informs us that as early as the year 1705 only a few of the people still retained a knowledge of the old Filipino method of writing. Thus it is that today only the more primitive of the Filipino peoples to whom we may properly refer as retaining a tribal organization, such as the Tagbanuas of the island of Palawan, continue to use the old-fashioned syllabic system of writing. Deeds of ancestors, songs about the dead and also about the numerous deities, poems and songs used while working or rowing, and their genealogies were the types of literature thus recorded.

If we must look to existing remnants of native Filipino tribal life for records of pre-Spanish literature, we must likewise turn to conservative Spanish elements in Filipino life for the preservation of Spanish culture and use of Spanish language. Thus the University of Santo Tomas in Manila, which is older than Harvard, continues as the bulwark of Spanish culture and speech against rapidly increasing use of American idioms. An influential element in the permanent foreign population of Manila is Peninsular Spanish, a fact that serves to reinforce the use of Spanish by those Filipinos of the more conservative and wealthy classes who received their education at the University of Santo Tomas in Manila. Up to a comparatively recent date most of the positions of authority and leadership in the Philippine Islands were in the hands of those possessing the Hispanic cultural outlook. Jurists, lawyers, the native secular clergy, physicians and, most important of all, the vociferous politician continued his use of Spanish even though the date for the change of the official language from Spanish to English had been set and long passed.

In its relations with the American people and its government the Filipino people has had a number of bewildering experiences. Many thousands of American men and women have been brought from the United States and assigned to duties in the insular and 48 provincial and subprovincial governments. The influx of American civil servants began in 1901 with the installation of a civil government. Even earlier, individual soldiers of the American Army had been assigned to teaching in

PLATE 17

1. A TINGLAYAN

The Tinglayans form a subdivision of the Bontoc peoples of north central Luzon, more than 25,000 in number. Their wavy hair, tall stature, and general appearance do not conform to the general Filipino physical type.

2. GROUP OF BATAKS, ISLAND OF PALAWAN

The Bataks are a pagan Negrito people numbering less than 1,000. They do not conform physically to the general Philippine Negrito type, resembling more the Andaman Islanders. They have retained much of their native culture. Note the woman's elaborate headdress.

PLATE 18

2. NEGRITO MAN, MARIVELES, PROVINCE OF BATAAN

Note beard and general resemblance to the West African Negro. His height is 4 feet 8 inches. The costume is typical

1. DEAN C. WORCESTER AND ADULT NEGRITO WOMAN, MARIVELES, PROVINCE OF BATAAN

The woman is of average height of female pygmy Negrito. Her skirt is not typical.

PLATE 19

NEGRITOS MAKING FIRE, MARIVELES, BATAAN PROVINCE

The bamboo fire saw is in general use throughout the Islands, as it is also elsewhere in Indonesia.

1. GADDANG WOMAN

The skirt is not typical. Variation exists in the dress of pagan mountain tribes; most completely clothed are the women of the Nabaloi and Bontoc.

2. GADDANG MAN

The Gaddang, both Christian and pagan, number about 40,000 and occupy a small area in Isabela Province, upper Cagayan Valley, north-central Luzon. The hand woven, tailored jacket is unique among Filipino mountain tribes.

PLATE 21

1. TAGBANUA WOMAN

The Pagan Tagbanuas occupy the mountainous interior of Palawan. Their culture is primitive; clothing for both men and women is limited to a bark breech clout. They are literate and use the ancient Filipino syllabary, reading and writing in vertical columns from top to bottom and from right to left.

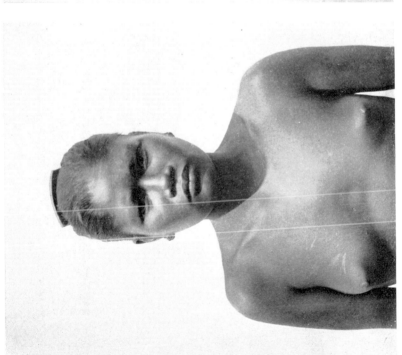

2. BONTOC-IGOROT MAN, NORTH-CENTRAL LUZON

Of all Filipino peoples, the pagan Bontoc-Igorot has aroused the most American interest. His independence and resourcefulness, irrigated rice-terrace agriculture, and reputation as a head hunter have obscured other remarkable and unique culture traits.

PLATE 22

2. TINGUIAN GIRL

The pagan Tinguian live in the province of Abra and adjoining regions of north Luzon. Both men and women wear long hair. The hairdress of the girl indicates she is unmarried.

1. KALINGA MAN

The pagan Kalinga lives in the subprovinces of Kalinga and Apayao, mountain province, and in the province of Cagayan, north central Luzon. He has been characterized as a rake.

2. TAGALOG WOMAN

She is a devout Christian and an excellent shopper. Significantly, she wears a black overskirt, the *tapis*, a rectangular cloth wrapped about the waist and worn over her skirt.

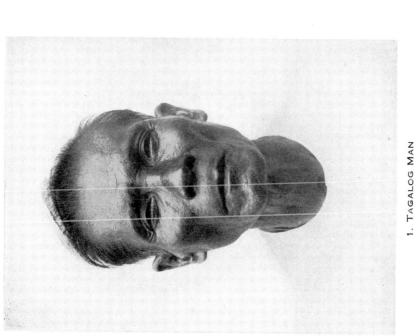

1. TAGALOG MAN

The numerically strong Tagalog people inhabit the rich agricultural valley of central Luzon and the environs of Manila Bay. Manila is a Tagalog city. The Tagalog had given up head hunting and become peaceful farmers and fishermen long before the arrival of the Spanish.

PLATE 24

FAMILY OF TAGALOG MAT WEAVERS. 1940

The weaving of mats, bags, and hats from the stripped leaves of the pandanus palm is a thriving household industry in the Tagalog town of Louisiana, Province of La Laguna, Luzon. Modern styles are reflected in the bobbed and curled hair of the girl in the center background, also in the tailoring of the women's calico print dresses. Conversely, the conventional manner of the Tagalog male of wearing his shirt tails loosely outside of his belt has been enthusiastically adopted by American youth. (Courtesy of the National Geographic Society.)

the provincial schools and to such duties of civil administration as could be conducted independent of the Army.

When convinced that further resistance to the American will was inexpedient, the Filipino lay down his weapons and cooperated with the American Army and later also with the civil government for the general good. His keen political judgment prompted him to adopt the American system in which he sensed honesty of purpose, leading to the enhancement of his economic and social order.

In overcoming the old problems, these newcomers, however, brought a number of new ones. Prior to the introduction of American sovereignty, the speech of the educated Filipino was that of his native provincial Indonesian dialect plus Spanish. Through more than 300 years of contact with Spaniards in government, in the church, in the school and in business, the Filipino learned to resort to Spanish in all dealing with the Spanish authorities and with Filipinos whose local speech was that of another province or island. Under American control, the official language and interprovincial communication became bilingual. Although English later became the official language of the schools, the courts, and the government, Spanish continued in use as the preferred language of the educated classes.

In forensics the use of English predominates, although under emotional stress a speaker may lapse into Spanish or even use his native Tagalog, Ilocano, or other provincial dialect.

The general use of English, which was a major principle of American colonial government, has made it possible to keep step linguistically with the nationalizing influence of a modern economic life. One may still hear fervent speeches in Spanish, also at times in one of the eight major Filipino dialects. English speech, however, has become the lingua franca of the leading Philippine ethnic groups. Tribal life among Christian Filipinos ceased when the political attitude of the Ilocano, Tagalog, the Visayan, and the several minor nationalities assumed a nation-wide scope. This transition began long before the arrival of the Americans. It had its origin in common economic, agrarian, and social grievances, but also in a common heritage of Christian doctrine and belief.

The influence of such culture innovations as have wrought great changes in speech of the peoples of other countries have also brought about the increased use of English, particularly in the cities. Reference is to the use of radio, the moving picture, and the automobile. It is, however, not readily explainable just why the Filipino has adopted the use of the English language newspaper when the wealthier classes of the established order certainly prefer the use of Spanish. The answer lies perhaps in the fact that American civilization introduced into the Philippine Islands something that did not exist before, namely, a numerous middle class. This class was drawn from the ranks of the impoverished peasant *tao* and city laborer, whose children received their education in the public schools where English was the official language. The use of English has served to unite the vast majority of Filipinos and cement their culture through the medium of common speech. The formerly disfranchised, illiterate, deeply indebted *tao* knew only his local dialect and therefore was ill adapted for success in city life or in the use of such talents for leadership as he may have possessed. In 1901, 509 American school teachers arrived in the Islands on the Army transport *Thomas,* and thereafter thousands of additional American teachers came for sojourns of 2 years or longer. The consequent introduction of the English language enabled the Filipino to grasp and put to immediate use such gadgets and accessories of western culture as came to the islands. The Filipina woman, long known as shrewd, economically stable, conservative, and not given to ebullient temperamental outbursts as is her more explosive spouse, has used to good advantage her newly acquired right to vote. In a recent election nearly 500,000 women voted. It may be assumed that many of these received stimulus to participate in civic affairs through perusal of their daily newspaper printed in the English language. Of the 15 daily newspapers published in Manila, the leading ones are in English, edited and managed entirely by Filipinos. There are 270 publications in the Islands with a total circulation of 1,500,000. More than one-half of these are printed in the English language.

The spread of the use of English is attested by the number of American magazines sold throughout the Islands. That many of these belong to the pulp variety makes no more and no less difference in the use of the king's English than it does in the United States, where the same magazines are found on the newsstands in every city. The Filipina woman studies American fashion magazines and revamps her costume accordingly. A certain amount of picturesqueness, to be sure, has been lost in the process, but the Filipina has been the gainer.

The spread of American slang has been blamed on sports and on the movies. Movies in air-cooled theaters and the Sampaguita pictures, a local Manila product, have become Philippine institutions. Manila in 1940 made about 50 films a year. A San Francisco-born Filipina is a favorite star. She had to memorize her lines when the script was in native Tagalog of which she could not understand a single word. The Filipino moviegoer has not progressed to the American's preference for gangster pictures. He is satisfied with a love story. It must not, however, have a tragic ending.

R. F. Barton remarks about the casual introduction of English words into the speech of the hill peoples, the Igorots, along with their adoption of new ideas and culture traits. Thus when the Igorot had occasion to refer to walking, he could draw on any number of Kankanai words and phrases to denote the various ideas of walking uphill, downhill, along a rice dike, and other types of walking. He had, however, no phrase giving exactly the English equivalent of merely taking a walk so that he lifted the phrase "take a walk" bodily from the English language and inserted it in the middle of a sentence encased with numerous native Kankanai prefixes and suffixes to indicate proper tense, mode, and other grammatical relations.

In communicating with native populations in the Islands, the Japanese invaders have found to their chagrin that use of English is indispensable. Japanese long resident in the Islands are more familiar with the local native Filipino dialect than Filipinos are with Japanese. Since Tagalog is spoken by approximately one-fourth of the population in the Philippine Islands and is understood by most Filipinos living in Manila and in the densely populated central valley of Luzon, the Japanese have declared Tagalog and Japanese the official languages of the Islands, hoping thereby to avoid the use of English.

THE BARANGAY AND THE STATE

In primitive Philippine society, as uninfluenced by Mohammedan culture or contacts with Spanish colonial government, the political unit is the village, the ancient Tagalog *barangay*, perpetuated in the modern barrio, the smallest political unit for which census data are published. A barrio may consist of from 10 to 1,000 houses. Ordinarily these habitations are located near each other, forming a small village. The barrio may consist of several adjoining settlements known as *sitios*. Typically one barrio is separated from another by rice fields (paddies). The centrally located barrio and the one in which the municipal building stands is known as the poblacion. Those Philippine ethnic groups or political units which were subjected to Mohammedan influence invariably were island-wide in scope with their powerful rajas and sultans. In ancient Indonesian Philippine society, on the contrary, each village thought of the population of other villages, even though speaking the same languages, as foreigners. In native Filipino life, therefore, we find originally a multitude of small communities each distrustful and independent of the other, with feuds either imminent or in progress. Politically and socially native Philippine society was thus truly feudal. The village *barangay* was small and embraced less than 100 families. The chief of the *barangay* was the *dato,* which in some areas in the Philippines was interchangeable with the term *raja,* a word derived from the language of India. A cluster of *barangays* resembling the modern *sitios* (suburbs) was loosely governed by a council composed of the respective village *datos.* The society's control over the individual under the *barangay* was complete. A young man could not set out to live in another *barangay* without the payment of money and the consent of the community. Feudal life flourished in the sense that individual wrongs were avenged by the community since the offense was considered as given not to the individual but to the community.

The *dato* or leader of the *barangay* was usually selected through his ability as a natural leader because of personal bravery or through wealth. Inasmuch as property in the form of land or other material objects could be inherited, the supposition is that the datoship passed through inheritance from father or mother to their children. Thus tribes of northern Luzon as yet uninfluenced by Spanish or other western political organization still retain this form of hereditary leadership. It is interesting to note that while the structure of society of the Ilocano and Tinguian differs in many respects from that of the Bontoc-Igorot and Ifugao, the political organization into *barangay* with similar hereditary leaders or chiefs was nevertheless characteristic of the Ilocano and Tagalog during the days of the early Spanish conquest, and is still characteristic of the Lepanto and Bontoc-Igorot at the present time. The obvious assumption is that observed differences drawn between the culture of the Ilocano and Tinguian on the one hand and the Bontoc-Igorot and Ifugao on the other are of recent chronological origin. Differences existing in the social organization of the Igorot peoples of northern Luzon on the one hand and of the neighboring Apayao, Kalinga, Tinguian, and Ilocano peoples on the other, may perhaps be more ancient. The division of Igorot settlements into village units known as the *ato* does not reappear in the social and political village units of the Apayao and other peoples named in the second group. The Igorot *ato* is joined to other *atos* of the village federation by a representative council of old men. The Apayao village, however, has a headman, aided by the elders of his village. The existence of a headman in the Apayao village and not in that of the Igorot, while each of the two contrasted social organizations has a council of old men, is a difference not sufficiently great to appear significant, since each falls well within the limit of variations in social structure common to Indonesia. It is perhaps due to the small area controlled by the *barangay* and its consequent weakness in manpower that first the Mohammedanized Moro and later the Spaniard were allowed to disrupt native Philippine society and to establish a political unit of larger dimension—either a *raja*-controlled state or a Christianized Spanish-controlled unit. Magellan in 1521 observed that the smaller chiefs in the Visayan Islands bore the title *raja* rather than *dato*. The fact that Magellan was actually killed when he sided with the *raja* of Cebu in his party feud with the *raja* of the nearby small island of Mactan leads us to believe that the Visayan *raja* controlled a *barangay* similar in extent to that of the ancient Tagalog *barangay* on the island of Luzon.

As in Mohammedan Malay society, in Jolo and eastern Mindanao, primitive Tagalog society had four classes. Beneath the ruling *dato* class were the people who were freed from the payment of tribute to the *dato*. However, as in feudal European society, this class had to render service to its chief as rowers of his boat, as warriors, and as personal attendants. The third class consisted of liberated slaves but who were required to give greater or heavier service than the free-born. This class attended to the routine agricultural duties and the tending of fishing and hunting. It also was compelled to perform any other tasks, the performance of which was requested by the *dato*. The slaves made up still a fourth class. The rights of slaves were nonexistent as is the case in all slave-holding societies. Captives in intervillage warfare, if their lives were spared, became slaves. Another class of slaves resulted from the incurrence of debt. A starving family receiving the loan of a few paddies of unhusked rice from a rich neighbor could, after a lapse of time, if the debt were not paid, become his slaves as long as the debt remained unpaid. Usurious interest charges were characteristic and remained a characteristic of Philippine society, so that as the debt remained unpaid and the interest accumulated, all hope of paying the original debt receded. The children of the parents who incurred the debt thus became by inheritance the slaves of the parents' creditor. This form of slavery has been persistent throughout various agricultural sections of the Philippine Islands. The number of children thus born into or retained in slavery depended on the amount of the original debt.

The foundation of the Malaysian civic organization is the family. On it—that is, on common descent—the great stems or tribes are built under various names but always with the same meaning. The Filipino family with all its *parientes* or relatives, retainers, and debt-induced servitors remains the active basis of modern native society in westernized or civilized Philippine communities. However, the following details relative to the ancient Malaysian *suka* are today applicable in the Philippines only to the pagan tribes.

The Malaysian *suka*, i.e., tribal associates, are traditional brothers, and often we find the tribe responsible for the misdeeds of its individual members. With this there goes the possibility of casting out undesirable members or associates. Within the group marriage is forbidden. Great family heads, and also greater or lesser tribal chieftains, stand at the head of the tribal subdivisions. As in the course of time the individual branches of every people become intermingled, the genealogical rule becomes divided and breaks down. In addition, there are territorial chiefs whose power is of more recent date. There we find often side by side tribal chieftains and village chiefs. As advisors of the chief, there are leaders in war and priests. This division of authority is found not only among the Mohammedan Malays but seems to be of older origin.

Typically Indonesian is the splitting up into innumerable small states (every village is an independent state) that are continuously engaged in feuds with one another. Larger unions were first introduced from India, and during the period of Hindu supremacy we find numerous larger, or even very large, kingdoms—characteristic examples of Asiatic dominion. Out of these there have arisen in the course of Mohammedan times— that is, within the past 500 years—the numerous sultanates that, starting with the possession of a small waterfront area, gradually came into the possession of the watershed of a large river or a harbor. The best known of such sultanates are the two kingdoms of Solo and Djogdja on the island of Java, and Asjeb, which at the time of its greatest extent embraced the entire northern half of Sumatra and even equipped great fleets against the Portuguese and Dutch and successfully waged war with them. At present all the sultanates have sunk to the level of small kingdoms— mere shadows of their former greatness.

Slavery and warfare, two institutions that formerly played a great role in the lives of these people, have under European rule been pushed more and more into the background. One may distinguish three kinds of slaves: those captured in war (here may be included simple theft), slaves through debt, and slaves by birth. The treatment of slaves generally is good; they are counted as belonging to the family of their master, but they have almost no rights, and their lives are at the disposal of their masters.

HEAD HUNTING AND HUMAN SACRIFICE

Institution of head hunting.—One of the most impelling motives of intertribal warfare among the savage pagan and also among the Moro tribes is the prestige that attaches to those who have been successful in battle. The strongest and bravest of the tribe are entitled to enjoy a special title, *mangani,* and to wear a special costume. Among the Bagobos, for example, a man who has killed two people is permitted to wear a chocolate-colored headband; if the number of his victims is four, he may don trousers of a blood-red hue; when the number of killings amounts to six, he is able to apparel himself completely in maroon clothing. The incentive to make raids on neighboring tribes and villages is enhanced by the desire of every able-bodied Bagobo man to become a *mangani;* the desire to collect loot and slaves supplies an auxiliary motive when no other exists. Mrs. M. C. Cole writes that

all Bagobo warriors are under the special protection of two spirits, Mandarangan and his wife, Darago. They bring success in battle and give to the victors loot and slaves, but in return for these favors they demand at certain times the sacrifice of a human being. The Government is trying to persuade these spirits to accept a pig in place of a human life. Near the coast they are willing to do so, but they are more particular in the less accessible places. Datu Tongkaling claims to have killed more than 30 of his enemies in fair fight and to have assisted in an even greater number of human sacrifices.

As with most primitive peoples, attacks are made only when some advantage will accrue to the attacker. Ambushes of various sorts are devised. At such times no distinction is made between the able-bodied fighting members of the tribe and the children or the old people. A head is a head, regardless. Head hunting was formerly as widely distributed as the Indonesian ethnic stock, from the Nagas of Assam across the Sunda Islands, the Moluccas, Formosa, and the Philippines. Certain symbols in the clothing of the Nagas indicate the number of captured heads; on the Mentawi Islands bodily tattoo marks increase with the accumulation of human heads. In certain areas in Luzon when a new family dwelling was to be constructed human sacrifices were in order, and enemy heads were selected and buried under the foundation posts. This custom was formerly practiced by the Batak, but more recently pieces of red cloth came to be substituted for the bloody heads. Among some tribes the captured heads were artificially prepared and. then hung up in the young men's dormitories.

Elsewhere in the interior of the Philippine Islands tribal units were always small and feuds were petty and continuous. Here, again, the rugged character of the terrain, especially in northern Luzon and in Palawan and in Mindoro, sufficed to keep the small political or tribal units from uniting. Often the local feuds and combats degenerated into a purely family undertaking. Among the Ifugao of northern central Luzon, who dwell south and east of the Bontoc-Igorot and northeast of the Benguet-Igorot, not even the authority of headmen was recognized. The population, however, is here especially dense, totaling over 100,000. Although the system of law worked out by the Ifugao is remarkable, the lack of competent authority still leads to perpetual feuds. The individual or family suffering an affront must seek its own revenge. If their retaliation should take the form of an excess number of deaths meted out to their adversary, their act led to additional encroachment on their lives and property, which called for additional retribution, and so the feud went merrily on.

Where customs differ from community to community, as among the Kalinga, who dwell north of the Bontoc and east of the Tinguian, the general name given to the many small groups, namely, *kalinga,* enemy, seems very appropriate. This loosely knit population of more than 50,000 equals the Ifugao in industry and in agricultural undertakings requiring united effort and the cooperation possible only under a system of law. But as late as the year 1940, after decades of American intervention, traces of their local feuds continue and private justice is the individual's last resort.

Throughout the Philippine Islands, and western Malaysia as well, the rule of private justice held sway. Head hunting as an institution was its chief manifestation. Although but one phase of a ceremonialism that demanded the severed head of an enemy or stranger for different occasions, the real source of the practice lay in the private enforcement of law. The victim may be any individual belonging to a tribal group other than the one to which the party seeking vengeance or a head trophy belongs. Among some pagan tribal groups in the Philippines, according to Dr. J. R. Harris, agricultural undertakings such as rice planting could not successfully be undertaken without a preliminary head-hunting expedition. Ceremonies of many sorts called for a number of recently severed enemy heads. Similar to the counting coup of the Plains Indian, the primitive Filipino warrior enjoyed increased esteem with each enemy head to his credit. After proudly displaying his bloody trophy, the head was hung permanently on the doorposts or on poles outside the house; sometimes the head was placed inside the house. This was a religious observance and provided safety to the dweller from the *anitos,* or evil spirits. The Bontoc-Igorot buried the head and sometimes employed the mandible of the skull as a gong handle.

Substitution of human sacrifice and blood money.—The penetration of the higher Indian and Arabic religions throughout the southern Philippine Islands caused the practice of head hunting to fall into disrepute. "Blood money" was substituted in its stead, and the evidence of a warrior's victories no longer was required to be placed on display. Marks on the side arms often indicated the number of victims the warrior had slain. At the time of the arrival of the Spaniards, head hunting was practiced much more extensively than at the time of the coming of the Americans. The Sambal, Ilocano, and the Cagayanes, all coast tribes of northern Luzon, have become Christianized and have given up the custom. The Tinguian and the Benguet-Igorot discontinued the practice at a late date. The American Philippine Constabulary found it necessary to force discontinuance of the practice by the Ifugao, Bontoc, Kalinga, and other pagan tribes of the mountainous interior of northern central Luzon. To bring this about, drastic action on the part of the constabulary was often necessary. This does not imply, however, that head hunting is completely stamped out. The force of peaceful example by those who have discontinued the practice is probably quite as effective as is armed force.

Two great civilized peoples, the Tagalog of central Luzon and the Visayas of Cebu, Leyte, Negros, Panay, etc., had discontinued taking heads of their own accord before the arrival of the Spaniards. The same applied to the Mohammedan tribes, likewise the Mindanao pagan Bagobo, Manobo, and Mandayan tribes; also to the Negritos of western Luzon. Among some the cutting off of the ears of their fallen foes sufficed. Sometimes the hair was clipped to provide tassel ornaments for belts and scabbards. Count was kept of the number of enemies killed. The courage of the warrior and the skill with which he wielded his weapons always aroused the respect and esteem of the individual in the group. It is true that every man intended to pay his debts, including such debts of honor as avenging a violent death suffered by one of his family or group. If he paid the "debt of life" with interest and exceeded the balance, additional reprisals were called for and the feud did not stop.

It is at this point that mercenary interests enter, and wherever a headman's authority is recognized, "blood money" is acceptable. At first money was proffered and accepted only where no intent to commit injury was present. As such the wrong was compoundable. When the institution of "blood money" gained entry within a group, feuds became subject to money settlement. As the chief received a portion of the sum for his share, his influence was all toward the suppression of blood feuds. The fact that he was able to suppress such difficulties between neighboring tribal groups increased his influence.

The pagan tribes of the southern islands had developed the practice of accepting blood money for human sacrifice, while the northern primitive tribes continued to take blood vengeance through head hunting. The Visayan islanders leaned toward the former practice, while Mohammedan influence tended to discontinue both practices among its devotees.

The pagan tribes of the mountain province of northern Luzon formerly made of head hunting a rite. This ceremonial religious observance

6

has to a great extent been suppressed by the Philippine Constabulary. Tribal warfare has likewise become a thing of the past. Trophies of battle consisting of the skulls of the slain enemies, however, still ornament the walls of the house of the pagan warrior. The severed heads of slain enemies were stuck by returning expeditions on a pole which had attached to it just beneath as a further ornament the horns of a water buffalo, sacred leaves, and other ceremonial objects. The heads were now supposed to lend their aid to the successful tribe and were treated with respect. A sacrificial feast followed upon the return of a head-hunting expedition, the dog or common carabao being the sacrificial offering.

Since the practical suppression of head hunting, which includes also a ban on the production of spears and other weapons employed by the head hunter, heads of sacrificial animals, or the horns of such animals, replace the wall trophies before alluded to.

RELIGION

Approximately 95 percent of the population of the Philippines are Christians with a modern outlook on life quite like that of the American people of today. In contrast are the Indonesians, Malays, and other ethnic stocks of the Dutch East Indies, of whom 95 percent have become proselytes of Islam and participants in the Mohammedan way of life. The first Filipino peoples to accept Christianity and the Catholic ritual were naturally those who occupied the great central valley of Luzon, the seaport towns, and the city of Manila. Agricultural peoples, in contact with western culture for more than 300 years, are the Tagalog of Manila and adjoining areas, the Pampanga and the Pangasinan of the central valley of Luzon, the Ilocano of northwestern Luzon, the Sambal of Bataan Peninsula, the Cagayan of the great valley of the Cagayan in northeast Luzon, the Bicol of southern Luzon, and the Visayan of the central islands of Panay, Negros, Bohol, Cebu, and Leyte. To the qualities of Spanish formal catholicism rich in appealing ceremony has been added a veneer of American protestantism. In many instances tenets of American Christian life have become more than a veneer to the cultured Filipino.

Irrespective of cultural influences from India or Spain, the substrata of religious belief is identical throughout the islands. The ancestral spirits who can work havoc or be of assistance during the entire lifetime of the individual must be propitiated or appeased. These spirits, the so-called *anitos,* are omnipresent and great precautions must constantly be taken not to offend them. Pigs and chickens were killed as sacrifices. A form of animism is strongly developed in pagan Filipino religion inasmuch as the spirits could be approached through living plants and animals. The crow and the crocodile were favorite mediums. Primitive Indonesian society is one of the most fear-ridden among the world's peoples because of the ever-present danger of dissatisfied and all-powerful *anitos*. Amulets, charms, and a nondescript *anting-anting* encased in a bag were carried as personal possessions by every individual. Where the powers that make for good or evil, according to the religious notions of the people, exist among the lesser galaxy of gods or spirits, the mere creator or maker of things assumes less importance. Thus native worship of the Tagalog deity Bathala, which is a word of Sanskrit origin, and Lumawig, the common designation for the deity throughout Malaysia, would not in itself dispel superstitious fears and imaginings.

Indonesian native religion rests basically upon two partly overlapping and partly independent sets of concepts, namely, generalized animistic beliefs regarding spirits of innumerable varieties, and ideas connected with the ancestor cult. Pantheons of beings higher than the hordes of minor spirits, as well as actual deities, function as integral parts of the ancient cults throughout most of Indonesia, but the great majority of these superior beings are otiose and receive little direct attention in ritual and sacrifice. In eastern Indonesia, however, from eastern Celebes and the Lesser Sundas to New Guinea, sky-earth dualism, usually involving pairs of celestial male and terrestrial female deities, rise to parallel the ancestor cult in significance, while the purely animistic spirit cult which predominates in most parts of western Indonesia, drops into a relatively minor position. Each of these major primitive religious concepts are represented in the Philippines as surviving beliefs underlying professed Christian beliefs and cults. Thus, when the people of Bontoc "felt afraid," they repaired to the crest of the ridge which separates the town of Bontoc from that of Talubin where a group of *anitos* is ranged beside the trail in order to prevent the people of the latter place from coming to Bontoc to hunt heads. Here they sacrificed chickens in a newly kindled fire, subsequently hanging the baskets in which they brought them upon a fencelike structure. The people of Talubin say it is very dangerous to pass this place and always make it a point to go around when possible.

Among the Ifugao the law of custom is the most commonly exercised standard of individual and group behavior although taboo based on religious beliefs is also invoked. An example of a taboo is the injunction against strangers passing near a rice field during harvest time, or entering a village when people are ceremonially idle. Although many taboos were arbitrary, and as such may be said to be derived from magic, most taboos are essentially reasonable—taboos against practices that in modern Filipino society would be covered by statutory law.

In pagan Filipino society the decision of battle is a judgment by the gods. Even less important disputes between families or individuals require, in the absence of a secular judge, judicial decisions based on traditional forms of ordeals or magic judgments. Thus, among the Ifugao, if two individuals mutually accuse each other, both are tried by ordeal. The application of heat in the form of a heated bolo or pebble reveals the judgment of the gods in more serious burns for the guilty than for the innocent.

The duel affords the Ifugao another traditional form of magic judgment. The weapons may be spears, reed stalks, or even eggs. Only eggs are used as weapons in a duel over accusation of adultery.

Myths are recited by the Ifugao in religious ceremonies as a means to magic. The myth is first recited by the priest. The myth selected is an appropriate one affording an analogy to the condition of sickness, famine, or other circumstance to be alleviated. Sympathetic magic is invoked in that the priest wills that the solution of the problem in hand be a similarly happy one to that developed in the myth. The priest next recalls the gods of the particular myth he has recited from their abode in the underworld or the sky world to retrace every step taken by them in their journeying, as mentioned in the myth, back to the particular Ifugao village where the ceremony is transpiring. The gods finally arrive and grant the recovery of the sick or grant benefits as requested. This is plain witchcraft.

Every Filipino is acquainted with the ancient Indonesian belief regarding the creation in which Lumawig the Supreme One (Bathala) created the sky, the sea, and the kite. This great bird, in flying closer to the sky, made the sea feel jealous.

In her jealousy, the sea threw up mighty waves against the sky. The sky did not like this and grew dark over the sea. The sea hurled her waves higher; she seethed and tossed, then suddenly she splashed the sky with brine. This embittered the sky, and he began to punish the sea. He showered rocks and earth on the water, until finally islands rose above the sea. In the end, the sea could only roll and break her waves upon the shores, and she has been doing this ever since. These islands are the Philippines.

The sea and the sky became reconciled again, and Lumawig in heaven was pleased. The kite, too, was glad. The renewed friendship of the two found its consummation in their devotion to the islands which had arisen out of their quarrel. Thus the sky was always fair over the Philippines, and the sea ever guarded its shores.

Such friendship must bear a greater fruit, said Lumawig. So he brought together the land-breeze and the sea-breeze on the islands. And the two winds met with the light from the sky and the rain from the sea, and in their meeting they caused bamboos to grow in the Philippines. One of these bamboos was unusually large, large enough to hold a man inside.

One day, when the sky was bright and the sea was calm, the kite went hunting for food in the bamboo groves. Catching a dragon fly, it lighted on the huge bamboo to finish its meal. Then it pecked the tree to clean its beak. And a voice inside the bamboo urged the bird to peck harder. The kite was frightened, but it wanted to know what was inside. Again the voice urged it to peck harder, and it did.

Finally, the bamboo split, and a man stepped out from the first joint, and a woman from the second. There had been nothing like them before, and the other creatures gathered around them to admire their beautiful forms. They called the man Silalak, and the woman Sibabay (*lalaki,* man; *babai,* woman).

Silalak loved Sibabay, and she returned his love. They became the first Filipino husband and wife. In time, the couple raised a big family, and nature was always good to them. They had vast fields of rice that yielded good harvests every year. But, when the children were full-grown and they saw the abundance of food around them, they began to be idle, and their father became angry at them. Silalak belabored his idle children with a stick, and they all ran in different directions to save themselves. Some went into the hidden rooms of the house, and from them were descended the leaders and headmen. Others ran out to the open fields, and they became the ancestors of the farmers. Still others went to hide under the house, and these became servants and laborers. Those who went far away became traders.

There were also many who made their way across the sea, and were not heard of for ages. Their children came back in the dawn of history, and they were the Indonesians, Malays, Hindus, Arabs, Chinese, and Japanese. The temperatures of the various regions in which they had lived had caused their skin to vary in color. The Spaniards and Americans, who had gone farthest from home, were the latest of all to come back.

This was all the will of Lumawig through the sky, the sea, and the kite.

Fundamental beliefs are embodied in Filipino songs and ballads; in the *dung-aw,* or loud lamentation, that is chanted upon the death of some one; in the invocations to the spirits; and in myths, legends, and folkways. In these musical, literary, and social forms are recounted the genealogies of deities, the great deeds of heroes, and the virtues of the dead.

One of the oldest customs is the worship of ancestors; for they feel indebted to those who have gone ahead, and believe that they are intercessors in the world beyond. To express veneration for ancestors, sacrifices and prayers to their spirits are offered, and their *ladawan,* or images, are carved in wood, stone, ivory, or metal.

Filipinos anciently believed that man, made of temporal substance, has an eternal soul. When death occurs, the soul undergoes a series of purifications before it can go to paradise. This is in the form of transmigrations—a sort of purgatory—in a cluster of 51 islands. First, the soul goes to an island where the trees, birds, rivers, and all other things are black. Then it passes to the other islands, on each of which all things are of a different color, and on which it receives punishments for the various sins that it has committed in life.

If it survives these punishments, the soul then attains purity and arrives at the last island, which is entirely white. This is paradise, where the pure and just enjoy perpetual youth and happiness. Here, the trees are always full of ripe fruits, and their roots are of gold. Of gold also is the wearing apparel: clothes, hats, shoes, bracelets, earrings, everything.

In this paradise are different flowers, including the *sampaguita,* the national flower of the Philippines. The seashore of this white island is of pure rice. There is a lake of sweet milk and another of *linugaw* (rice boiled with milk). Another stream is of blood, on the banks of which are plants, with flowers whose petals are flesh ready for eating. Such is the pagan Filipino paradise, where only the pure and just can reside.

Death and burial.—Extensive practices and customs are finally connected with death and burial. Lamenting women or the nearest female relatives sing long songs of lamentation, often with an ancient text, and tear their hair and scratch themselves. The belief is that the souls of the departed dead wander about restlessly until the burial festivities. There are many regulations to observe. Among the Mohammedan natives, burial is according to Mohammedan custom. Among pagan peoples the most varied customs prevail. With the transfer of the coffin to its final resting place, be it in the village or in front of the village, great festivities and banqueting are in order. Formerly, it was customary, according to the position or rank of the dead person, to make human sacrifices, a custom disseminated throughout the whole of Indonesia. Burial itself varies. One form is a burial in the ground, another a preservation of the coffin above the ground. Widespread is the burial in wooden coffins shaped like boats, as among the Moros of Mindanao and the Dyaks in Borneo. The beautifully ornamented larger or smaller ossuary houses in which after many years the remnants of bones are preserved have almost entirely disappeared from the land of the pagan Filipino, while his spirit world and ancient deities syncretize with those of the West.

SUMMARY

Of all the peoples of Asia and of the Indonesian island world off its southeastern coast, those living under the banner of the Commonwealth of the Philippines stand alone as beneficiaries of the cultural heritage of the Western world and of the civilizations brought to the Islands from Eastern lands.

The peoples of the Philippines have not shared equally in their inheritance. One of them, the diminutive, woolly-haired, black Negrito, who roams the forested uplands of Bataan and the eastern slopes of the axial cordillera, has been content to borrow from his immediate neighbor a working vocabulary and also those traits of material culture that suited his meager requirements for survival.

Another ethnic element consisting of an entire group of Igorot peoples living in northern Luzon, namely, the Bontoc, Kankanai, Nabaloi, Ifugao, and Ilongot, have preserved a number of ancient Indonesian institutions, similar to those tenaciously retained by the so-called proto-Malayans of the greater Sunda Islands of Sumatra, Java, Borneo, and Celebes. These institutions pertain more to the structure of their society than to their means of obtaining a livelihood and include separate communal dormitories for unmarried men and boys, also for unmarried women and young girls. The associated practice of trial marriage and pre-marital promiscuity contrasts starkly with marriage and family life elsewhere in the Islands. The inflexible organization of Igorot villages into wards or *ato* with the headmen forming a governing council is in contrast with the *barangay* or ancient primitive village organization of other Filipino peoples. The houses of the Igorot are built with flooring and siding of hewn planks of the mountain pine; elsewhere in the Islands, house construction is essentially of bamboo and rattan. Then, too, these Igorot mountain people—the Bontoc, Kankanai, Nabaloi, Ifugao, and Ilongot—are physically a sturdy lot. In contrast with the smaller-boned, more refined Filipino of the lowlands, or even with neighboring mountain peoples such as the Tinguian, Kalinga and Apayao, his body is sturdier, his legs shorter, nose broader, but head appreciably narrower.

The cultural peculiarities of these peoples of northern Luzon when considered along with their distinguishing physical characteristics have induced some American anthropologists, following the example of European scholars, to classify them as members of a subracial stock tentatively designated as "Indonesian," or, more conservatively, as indicating a very ancient migration "wave."

Since the true Malay has not migrated to the Islands in great numbers or in "waves," it is erroneous to characterize the Filipino as a "Malayan" people, even though he has adopted many Hinduized Malayan culture traits brought to the Islands. In this paper the use of the geographic term "Indonesian" has therefore been extended as the racial designation for all brown-skinned, straight-haired and black-haired Filipino peoples of the 50 political units or provinces enumerated in the 1939 census, including all of the 42 or more basic Indonesian dialects spoken by as many distinct ethnic groups throughout the archipelago.

Much of the prevailing variation in speech dialect and culture trait may be explained by the natural ruggedness of the country and the lack of natural highways. The high mountains separating the narrow valleys made the maintenance of trails difficult. The numerous islands separated by open water raised many barriers to free communication. Thus, settlements became self-contained and developed an independent speech dialect.

Primitive Filipino Indonesian society has inherited certain culture trait complexes, such as the practices of head hunting and slave taking, which anciently brought each settlement into a state of feud with other settlements. These practices, tending on the one hand to retard communication of ideas, also tended among the non-Christian peoples to conserve native Indonesian culture traits such as tattooing of the body and face and the mutilation of teeth by both sexes. The aversion to untreated teeth as being similar to those of a dog was widespread in the Indonesian Philippine and Sunda Islands. The corner edges of canine and incisor teeth were generally removed; more rare was the chipping of individual teeth to a point by means of a chisel and hammer. Even this Indonesian practice was to some extent imitated by the Negrito, who could not, however, because of his skin color tattoo his body. Cicatrization, or the raising of scar tissue, as elsewhere among black-skinned peoples, was resorted to by the Negrito to decorate his skin permanently. Although some Filipino peoples formerly blackened the teeth with tanbark and iron salts, the current practice of chewing the areca nut and betel leaf sprinkled with lime tends to produce a similar effect.

The elementary costume of the pagan Filipino for the male is the girdle and woven or bark fiber breech clout; for the female, the girdle and short wrap-around skirt, *lufid,* of woven cotton or bark fiber, open at the side.

The primitive *lufid,* the skirt of the pagan Bontoc woman, survives as the *tap'-is*—a dark-colored, generally black, skirt, open at the side or in front, extending from the waist to below the knees—a garment traditionally worn by the Christianized Tagalog, Ilocano, and Bikol women of Luzon, as well as elsewhere in the archipelago. The Igorot of Ilocos Sur and of Lepanto-Bontoc provinces, and the Tinguian women, also some Ilocano women of the Ilocos provinces, wear the *tap'-is* as the sole nether garment. Thus the *lufid,* the primitive Bontoc skirt, has survived as the *tap'-is,* a purely decorative, less ample and functionally useless conventional overskirt, for three centuries, even after the wearer dons beneath it several European garments, such as white underskirts and an overskirt.

Although in times of personal crises the pagan Filipino may still resort to the practice of sympathetic magic and to witchcraft, 95 percent of the population, nominally Christian or Mohammedan, invokes the aid of the Church or Koran. The *anting-anting* and other personal charms are, however, still worn to ward off the ill will of *anitos* and other gods of the spirit world. The creator, Bathala, survives for the most part only in folklore and story.

Beginning at an early period and continuing long after the original dispersal of the various ethnic stocks throughout the Islands we find a succession of cultural influences from abroad. Cultural influences emanating from India through the agencies of trade, religious missionaries, and the casual immigration of Hinduized Malays have penetrated to every Filipino people and settlement. Tavera has traced the survival of hundreds of words of Indian Sanskrit origin.

The primitive Filipino computed time and measured space with a system of numbers introduced by way of intermediate stages from India. With numerous alterations along the way, there came from the same source the alphabet or, more correctly, the syllabary. In the Islands the native development of the syllabic alphabet may be noted in the surviving examples of its use among the primitive Tagbanua of Palawan. The Indonesian shadow-play theater with its ancestral *wayang,* marionette figurine actors, brass gong beating, accompanied by the chanting or reciting of epic drama and stylized dancing originally was derived from Buddhistic India. This interesting chapter in the history of the drama has unfortunately been abruptly closed by the advent of the moving picture, even in Moro land where the Indonesian theater feebly survives.

In art designs the Filipino has drawn widely on environmental plant forms and animal life to produce beautifully executed leaf and floral patterns in wood carving or in cast, filigree, or inlay metal work. *Anito* spirit and ancestral *wayang* figurine carvings, as well as stylized zoomorphic dog and leech figurine designs, are characteristic of native Indonesian Filipino art, while the lotus blossom and leaf, emblematic of Buddhist symbolism, supplied a later design pattern throughout the Islands. Christian symbolism and art patterns were, of course, introduced by the Spanish friars in schools and in church architectural detail, principally in wood carving. Decorative design motives of pure Buddhist religious symbolism are found grafted on purely Indonesian design patterns. An Indonesian *wayang* figurine, for example, is carved on the pommel of the Visayan *barong* or bolo, while a conventionalized or stylized lotus pattern decorates the wooden scabbard. The art of metalwork, particularly in iron, was widely disseminated in the Islands even before the arrival of the Spaniards, and reveals Indian influence as having penetrated much more deeply than the comparatively recent protohistoric influence of Islam. The casting of brass and bronze, an art introduced from Borneo by the Mohammedan Malay, is best exemplified in the manufacture of the *lantaca,* a small cannon, by the Moro of Cottabato, in western Mindanao.

The influence of early sea-borne trade is illustrated by the surviving Chinese trade articles such as porcelain jars and stoneware, brass gongs, and weapon parts, and a vast array of other material objects. Chinese influence was limited to trade goods and left no impression on native Indonesian Filipino society.

Christian symbolism carved in wood in the many Catholic churches throughout the Islands is activated in the daily lives of the Filipino population. Unity, even within a province where no language barrier existed, would have been impossible without the deep penetration of Christian belief and doctrine. Much less could national unity within the Commonwealth have been attained. The disintegrating forces of intervillage feuding were not overcome until the Spanish friar and colonial administrator with ritual and the sword brought peace. Entire populations were parceled out as the property of a single Spaniard. Within this encomienda, so called, the Catholic orders established a church and a parochial school. Attracted by the color of the ritual of the Church and by the obviously superior civilization of the Spaniard, the Filipino was not unwilling to be baptized, to have his children taught in the schools, and to pay a share of all that he produced to the encomiendero and to the Church orders. He thus obtained cessation from petty feuding, a new and superior religion, and the way was opened to amicable intercourse with other Filipinos who lived beyond the confines of his ancestral village *barangay.* By 1896, when he finally and successfully revolted against the established Spanish regime, he had achieved a national unity that far exceeded the boundaries of any single native dialect. He had now reached the stage, thanks to the Spaniards, where he could read his own Mass and himself attend to the clerical duties of the tax collector. He had reached a degree of literacy, thanks to the humble Spanish parochial priest, superior to that of many peoples of Europe. He had written his own constitution for a Republic of the Philippines which he had created, with the capital city established in Malolos, in the Province of Bulacan, while he confined the Spaniards under siege within the city of Manila.

The American interlude, which immediately followed and which was brought to a close by the act of the Congress of the United States which established the Commonwealth of the Philippines, as outlined in this paper under the heading "American Contacts," has further consolidated Philippine political and cultural unity. The official language is now bilingual—Spanish and English. To Spanish catholicism has been added American protestantism. Mass education in public schools established throughout the entire archipelago has aided in building up a semi-independent middle-class citizenry out of the old debt-ridden semislave share-cropper. This newly enfranchised majority, along with the mestizo and economically independent minorities, look to the United States to remove the economic restrictions that gradually curtail and after 1946 entirely abolish, trade preferences in Philippine exports to the United States.

SELECTED BIBLIOGRAPHY

Arnold, Julean H.
　　1901. The peoples of Formosa. Smithsonian Misc. Coll., vol. 52, No. 3, pp. 287-293, pls. 19-22.

Barrows, D. P.
　　1905. A history of the Philippines. Indianapolis.

Barton, R. F.
　　1919. Ifugao law. Univ. California Publ. in Amer. Archeol. and Ethnol., vol. 15, No. 1, pp. 1-186, pls. 1-33.
　　1922. Ifugao economics. Univ. California Publ. in Amer. Archeol. and Ethnol., vol. 15, No. 5.

Bean, Robert Bennett.
　　1908. The Benguet Igorots. A somatologic study of the live folk of Benguet and Lepanto-Bontoc. Philippine Journ. Sci., vol. 3, No. 6, pp. 413-472, 8 pls.

Benedict, Laura W.
　　1916. A study of Bagobo ceremonial, magic, and myth. Ann. New York Acad. Sci., vol. 25.

Beyer, H. Otley.
　　1917. Population of the Philippine Islands in 1916. Manila.
　　1921. The Philippines before Magellan. Asia, vol. 21, pp. 861-866, 890, 892, 924-928.

BEYER, H. OTLEY, and BARTON, ROY FRANKLIN.
    1911. An Ifugao burial ceremony. Philippine Journ. Sci., vol. 6, No. 5,
        pp. 227-252, pls. 1-10.
BLAIR, E. H., and ROBERTSON, J. A.
    1903-1909. The Philippine Islands: 1493-1803. Vols. 1-55. Cleveland.
BLUMENTRITT, FERDINAND.
    1882. Versuch einer Ethnographie der Philippinen. Mit einer Karte der
        Philippinen. 69 pp. (Ergänzungsheft No. 67 zu Petermann's Mit-
        theilungen.) Justus Perthes, Gotha.
    1901. List of the native tribes of the Philippines and of the languages
        spoken by them. Ann. Rep. Smithsonian Inst., 1899, pp. 527-547,
        pls. 1-10.
CENSUS OF THE PHILIPPINE ISLANDS, 1903.
    1905. Vol. 1, Geography, history, and population. Washington.
CENSUS OF THE PHILIPPINES, 1939.
    1940. 5 vols. Manila.
CHRISTIE, E. B.
    1909. The Subanuns of Sindangan Bay. Bur. Sci., Div. Ethnol. Publ., vol. 6,
        No. 1, 29 pls. Manila.
COLE, FAY-COOPER.
    1908. The Tinguian. Philippine Journ. Sci., vol. 3, No. 4, pp. 197-213, 9 pls.
    1912. Chinese pottery in the Philippines. Field Mus. Nat. Hist., Publ. 162,
        vol. 12, No. 1.
    1913. The wild tribes of Davao District, Mindanao. Field Mus. Nat. Hist.,
        Anthrop. Ser., vol. 12, No. 2.
    1915. Traditions of the Tinguian. Field Mus. Nat. Hist., Anthrop. Ser.,
        vol. 14, No. 1.
    1922. The Tinguian, social, religious, and economic life of a Philippine
        tribe. Field Mus. Nat. Hist., Anthrop. Ser., vol. 14, No. 2.
CRAIG, AUSTIN.
    1913. Lineage, life and labors of Jose Rizal, Philippine patriot. 287 pp.
        World Book Co., Yonkers-on-Hudson, N. Y.
FINLEY, JOHN P., and CHURCHILL, WILLIAM.
    1913. The Subanu. Studies of a sub-Visayan mountain folk of Mindanao.
        Carnegie Inst. Washington, Publ. No. 184, pp. 1-236, 2 maps.
FORBES, WM. CAMERON.
    1929. Philippine Islands. Houghton Mifflin Co., Boston.
GARVAN, JOHN M.
    1940. The Manobos of Mindanao. Mem. Nat. Acad. Sci., vol. 23, No. 1,
        pp. 1-265, 14 pls. Senate Doc. No. 123, 77th Congr., 1st Sess.
        Washington.
HORN, FLORENCE.
    1941. Orphans of the Pacific. Reynal and Hitchcock, New York.
JENKS, A. E.
    1905. The Bontoc Igorot. Ethnol. Surv. Publ., Dep. Int., vol. 1, pp. 1-266,
        155 pls. Manila.
KRIEGER, HERBERT W.
    1926. The collection of primitive weapons and armor of the Philippine
        Islands in the U. S. National Museum. U. S. Nat. Mus. Bull. 137,
        pp. 1-128, frontispiece (map), pls. 1-21.

KROEBER, A. L.
1928. Peoples of the Philippines. Amer. Mus. Nat. Hist., Handbook Ser. No. 8, pp. 1-245, maps, figs. 1-44.

LAUFER, B.
1907. The relations of the Chinese to the Philippine Islands. Smithsonian Misc. Coll., vol. 50 (Quart. Issue, vol. 4, pt. 2), pp. 248-284.

MACKINLAY, W. E. W.
1905. A handbook and grammar of the Tagalog language. War Dep. Doc. No. 260, pp. 1-264. Washington.

MASON, OTIS T.
1907. Basketry bolo case from Basilan Island. Proc. U. S. Nat. Mus., vol. 33, pp. 193-196.
1908. Vocabulary of Malaysian basketwork: a study in the W. L. Abbott collections. Proc. U. S. Nat. Mus., vol. 35, pp. 1-51, pls. 1-18, figs. 1-41.
1909. Anyam Gila (mad weave): a Malaysian type of basket work. Proc. U. S. Nat. Mus., vol. 36, pp. 385-390.

MERRILL, E. D.
1926. A discussion and bibliography of Philippine flowering plants. Bur. Sci., Pop. Bull. 2. Manila.

MEYER, A. B.
1899. The distribution of the Negritos in the Philippine Islands and elsewhere. Dresden.

MILLER, EDWARD Y.
1905. The Bataks of Palawan. Ethnol. Surv. Publ., vol. 2, pt. 3, pp. 179-189, 6 pls. Manila.
1905. The Tugda, or rice planter, of the Coyunos, Philippine Islands. Smithsonian Misc. Coll., vol. 47 (Quart. Issue, vol. 2, pt. 3), pp. 375-376, pls. 51, 52.

MILLER. MERTON L.
1911. The non-Christian people of Ambos Camarines. Philippine Journ. Sci., vol. 6, sect. D, pp. 321-325, 4 pls. Manila.
1912. The Mangyans of Mindoro. Philippine Journ. Sci., vol. 7, sect. D, pp. 135-156, 10 pls. Manila.

MORGA, A. DE.
1868. The Philippine Islands, Moluccas, Siam, Cambodia, Japan and China at the close of the 16th century. Hakluyt Soc. Works (No. 39). London.

MOSS, C. R.
1920. Nabaloi law and ritual; Kankanay ceremonies. Univ. California Publ. in Amer. Archeol. and Ethnol., vol. 15, Nos. 3 and 4.
1924. Nabaloi tales. Univ. California Publ. in Amer. Archeol. and Ethnol., vol. 17, No. 5, pp. 227-353.

PENDLETON, ROBERT L.
1942. Land utilization and agriculture of Mindanao, Philippine Islands. Geogr. Rev., vol. 32, No. 5, pp. 180-210, 56 figs. New York.

PHILIPPINE JOURNAL OF SCIENCE.
1906-1941. Vols. 1-4, sect. A; vols. 5- , sect. D. Bur. Sci., Manila.

PLEYTE, C. M.
1891. Sumpitan and bow in Indonesia. Internat. Arch. Ethnogr., vol. 4, pp. 265-281, 4 pls. Leiden.

PORTER, RALPH S.
  1903. A primer and vocabulary of the Moro dialect. (Magindanau, etc.)
        Pp. 1-77. Government Printing Office, Washington.
REED, W. A.
  1905. Negritos of Zambales. Ethnol. Surv. Publ., vol. 2, pt. 1, pp. 1-90,
        62 pls. Manila.
ROOT, ELIHU.
  1901. The people of the Philippines. Letter from the Secretary of War.
        Senate Doc. No. 218, 56th Congr., 2d Sess. Washington.
SALEEBY, N. M.
  1905. Studies in Moro history, law, and religion; the history of Sulu. Bur.
        Sci., Div. Ethnol. Publ., vol. 4, Nos. 1-2, pp. 1-391. Manila.
SCHEERER, OTTO.
  1905. The Nabaloi dialect. Ethnol. Surv. Publ., vol. 2, pt. 2, pp. 97-173.
        Manila.
  1908. The Batan dialect as a member of the Philippine group of languages.
        Bur. Sci., Div. Ethnol. Publ., vol. 5, pp. 1-131, folded diagrams.
        Manila.
SIMPICH, FREDERICK.
  1940. Return to Manila. Nat. Geogr. Mag., vol. 78, No. 4, pp. 409-451,
        21 pls., map.
SKEAT, W. W.
  1903. The wild tribes of the Malay Peninsula. Ann. Rep. Smithsonian Inst.,
        1902, pp. 463-478, 2 pls.
SMITH, WARREN D.
  1908. A geologic reconnaissance of the Island of Mindanao and the Sulu
        Archipelago. Philippine Journ. Sci., vol. 3, No. 6.
  1924. Geology and mineral resources of the Philippine Islands. Manila.
SULLIVAN, L. R.
  1918. Racial types in the Philippine Islands. Amer. Mus. Nat. Hist.,
        Anthrop. Pap., vol. 23, pt. 1.
VANOVERBERGH, MORICE.
  1916. A grammar of Lepanto Igorot as it is spoken at Bauko. Bur. Sci., Div.
        Ethnol. Publ., vol. 5, pp. 331-425. Manila.
  1933. Philippine Negrito culture: independent or borrowed? Catholic An-
        throp. Conf., vol. 6, No. 2, pp. 25-35. Washington.
VENTURELLO, MANUEL HUGO.
  1907. Manners and customs of the Tagbanuas and other tribes of the Island
        of Palawan, Philippines. (Translated from the original Spanish
        manuscript by Mrs. Edw Y. Miller.) Smithsonian Misc. Coll.,
        vol. 48 (Quart. Issue, vol. 3, pt. 4), pp. 514-558.
VIRCHOW, RUDOLF.
  1901. The peopling of the Philippines. Ann. Rep. Smithsonian Inst., 1899,
        pp. 509-526, 3 pls.
WORCESTER, DEAN C.
  1906. The non-Christian tribes of northern Luzon. Philippine Journ. Sci.,
        vol. 1, No. 8, pp. 791-875, pls. 1-67. Manila.
  1912. Headhunters of northern Luzon. Nat. Geogr. Mag., vol. 23, No. 9.
  1913. The non-Christian peoples of the Philippine Islands. Nat. Geogr.
        Mag., vol. 24, No. 11.